My Life on a Hillside Allotment

www.**books**at**transworld**.co.uk

My Life on a Hillside Allotment

Terry Walton

BANTAM PRESS

LONDON • TORONTO • SYDNEY • AUCKLAND • JOHANNESBURG

TRANSWORLD PUBLISHERS
61–63 Uxbridge Road, London W5 5SA
a division of The Random House Group Ltd
www.booksattransworld.co.uk

First published in Great Britain
in 2007 by Bantam Press
a division of Transworld Publishers

Copyright © Terry Walton 2007
Illustrations by Stephanie Von Reiswitz

Terry Walton has asserted his right under the Copyright, Designs
and Patents Act 1988 to be identified as the author of this work.

This book is a work of non-fiction based on the life, experiences
and recollections of Terry Walton. The author has stated to the
publishers that the contents of this book are true.

A CIP catalogue record for this book
is available from the British Library.

ISBN 9780593057247

Addresses for Random House Group Ltd companies outside the UK
can be found at: www.randomhouse.co.uk
The Random House Group Ltd Reg. No. 954009

The Random House Group Ltd makes every effort to ensure that the
papers used in its books are made from trees that have been legally
sourced from well-managed and credibly certified forests. Our paper
procurement policy can be found at: www.randomhouse.co.uk/paper.htm

Typeset in 11½/15 pt Berkeley Book by
Falcon Oast Graphic Art Ltd.

Printed and bound in Great Britain by
Mackays of Chatham, Chatham, Kent.

2 4 6 8 10 9 7 5 3 1

To my dad, who introduced me to allotment gardening and has given me fifty years of a wonderful pastime. Thanks to his wisdom and knowledge I have lived a fulfilled life and enjoyed every moment of it.

Contents

Contents

Acknowledgements

First I should like to thank my wife, Anthea, for being an 'allotment widow' for forty years and allowing me the freedom to garden on a Rhondda hillside. Her patience and understanding have helped me enjoy my pastime, and the wonderful meals she has prepared from the produce have made my life a perfect joy.

Thanks to my two sons, Anthony and Andrew, for persuading me to join the media. Without them this book would never have been written. Thank you both for sharing your childhood with my allotment.

To Andi Clevely, who got up weekly to make the trek across from Llanidloes to Tonyrefail to make this book happen. Never mind, Andi, I'm sure the sunrises over the Brecon Beacons were a great reward.

To Jeremy Vine for the foreword, and for all the pleasant times we have shared on air bringing the allotments into the homes of his listeners. His show launched my new career in the media and has given my life an exciting new direction. Special thanks must go to Jessica Rickson for 'discovering' me and for being brave enough to recommend me for the Jeremy Vine allotment spot.

To Diana Beaumont, for giving me the opportunity to write this book, and to Sally Gaminara for teasing out my long-standing allotment stories and reawakening my brain cells.

To all the very nice and helpful staff at Transworld for all their hard work and help in creating this book, and to Ian Tripp, a fellow valley boy, for his local support.

To Albie for all his coffee and a place to meet on the allotments, and to all my fellow allotmenteers for their support and knowledge passed down over the years. I hope any budding allotment keepers out there will take the plunge and grab a plot, the starting point to a whole new way of life.

To my granddaughter, Megan, who has added a new dimension to my life and has brought even more love and happiness to an already contented man.

Foreword
by Jeremy Vine

Mostly, news ain't much fun. Whenever someone says to me, 'Why don't you report the trains that run on time?' I come over all queasy and mumble something about news being all the things we do not expect to happen (come to think of it, maybe that includes punctual trains). The day an accident-free factory or a sober judge is the top item on the news, we know we've had it. So programmes are packed to the rafters with what doesn't normally happen. Yes, it is big news in Houston when their underground system moves people successfully from one station to another, but that is because they do not have an underground system.

I suppose it's a good enough argument to justify what we do. I say 'suppose', with a bit of doubt and the stomach rumble that suggests the queasiness coming on again, because we all know what the end result is – news gets you down. News is things going wrong. A Martian who landed and tuned in to Alan Dedicoat would fire up the reverse boosters and get the hell out of here; sorry, Deadly, but you know what I mean. Just when your personal life is in balance, when you're looking out of the window of your home at a burst of autumn sunlight on the picket fence and thinking all's well with your family and friends, you switch on the radio and hear about bird flu or a nuke in a briefcase or some hurtling asteroid that is about to turn Manchester into a pancake. We don't exactly specialize in the brighter side of life.

All of which is to explain why we went in search of Terry Walton on Radio 2. We did not know he existed, of course. No one could guess the existence of the other TW without meeting him first. It was soon after the Iraq War began and the programme was full of blood and thunder. One afternoon, just when things couldn't get much more gruelling, we went local with a special on allotments and got the most phenomenal response. Thousands of calls, all asking about the really important things – How do you stop rabbits eating your lettuce? What's the best way to grow corn-on-the-cob? – as if from sheer relief that a complicated horror had given way to simple joys.

'Let's adopt our own allotment,' the editor Phil Jones suggested. We appealed for a plot on air. Producer Jessica Rickson trawled through the phone numbers of the dozens of allotmenteers who responded. And eventually she came back to me.

'There's a guy in the Rhondda, he's hilarious.'

'Does he have a mobile phone?' I asked.

'He has a phone and it works on his patch of land and he says he can garden live on air for us,' replied the efficient Jess, one step ahead as ever. 'But he says he's not for Bluetooth.'

Somebody once told me that broadcasting was genetic. You can either do it or you can't. I had always assumed the opposite: it's a skill you practise, like playing the clarinet, and when you practise you get better. Terry proved me wrong. From his debut, from the very first millisecond he appeared on the programme – which was, let's remember, the first bit of broadcasting he had ever done – he was one hundred per cent the finished article. It was wondrous to hear, like unleashing a whirlwind on the air! A real person, talking about something he loved! From that moment we knew we had a star on our hands.

Over time, I got to know Terry properly. During the 2005

general election we managed to shape the Radio 2 election journey around a visit to the allotment, and despite nearly falling for the famous 'These strawberries have just ripened today' joke (which you'll read about in the book), I left thinking we had connected with a genuine and lovely man whose on-air appearances were only an extension of his normal week and thus the perfect antidote to all the miseries of everyday news. Terry fights the woe with his hoe, and he has proved his credentials time and again . . . even driving miles to help listeners whose fruit and vegetables are foundering, striking the allotment equivalent of Control-Alt-Delete to get them restarted.

The Walton story is captivating in the same way his broadcasts are. His early childhood and dalliance with serious crime (well, blackcurrant scrumping); the 42-plot allotment where newcomers 'start at the far corner' and gradually move down, surely a parable for life; that picture he paints of the local cobbler working from a shed in his back garden. I never thought I would get so wrapped up in the origins of the Glamorgan Association of Allotments or keen to know the reason nobody in the Rhondda grew leeks, but Terry has grown us a blooming pageturner here! As befits a man who got his first plot in 1957 (for thirty-five pence a week), and seems only to have lost his temper once, in 1968, the book is full of practical, calm advice.

Anthea and Terry became grandparents just as I became a dad. They had Megan; Rachel and I were blessed with Martha. He sometimes tells me he regrets working so hard in the scientific instruments business when his two sons were young, and now he's determined to give Megan all the attention they missed out on. After a show one day, on one of his rare visits to London – yes, he did need oxygen for the trip – we had lunch at the local Italian round the back of Broadcasting House. Listening to him speak about work and family, decoding the implicit warning to a new father, I reflected that the benefits of Walton Wisdom extend way beyond the growing of vegetables into life in general.

For that reason I think I can guarantee you'll enjoy the story that follows, whether or not you have any interest in compost acidity or greenfly netting or the purples in a beetroot or any of the ordinary wonders Terry marvels at on our behalf. And if for any reason it's not your cup of tea, Terry being Terry, he will probably come to your home with a boxful of fresh parsnips to make it up to you.

Introduction:
The Adopted Allotment

It was 1 July 2003 when Phil Jones, the producer of BBC Radio 2's *Jeremy Vine Show*, rang me up to say, 'You're on on Friday!'

There are a few notable dates in life you always remember, aren't there? You know the day you were born, and you never forget the day you got married, nor the dates when your children were born. And this was another of those life-changing moments.

It had all started some time earlier, back in April 2003. My wife Anthea regularly listens to Radio 2, and it so happened that day that my older son, Anthony, was also tuned in. They both heard Jeremy Vine present an hour-long special on allotments. I didn't hear it because I was up on my own plot, on the side of the Rhondda valley in south Wales where I've been gardening for more than half a century, man and boy.

I'd rather be on my allotment than anywhere else I can think of. My plot has always been my passion and joy (as well as my constant source of good food), and it's been the theme running through my life since I first opened my eyes in the hospital maternity unit just the other side of the allotment fence. This book is the story of my gardening life there. It began in earnest when I was just four years old and starting to help my father regularly on his plot, on the same site and very close to the house where I was born. And I'm still up there, sowing and planting and harvesting, only now I share it with all the listeners to Jeremy Vine's radio show.

Towards the end of that allotment special, Jeremy announced he'd had a tremendous response from listeners, who were all ringing in with comments and questions, and the amount of interest was brilliant. Maybe it was only meant tongue-in-cheek, but he then added that he ought to get out of the studio more and perhaps have an allotment of his own. Was there anybody out there who would like to share their allotment with him and other listeners?

I knew nothing of this, of course. But when I came back home, first Anthea told me what Jeremy Vine had said and then Anthony rang me up and said I ought to write in, seeing as I was up there every single day.

My immediate reaction was a firm 'No!' Much as I enjoyed being out on the plot, I had always felt that allotments and radio simply weren't compatible. How could you have a show about allotments on the radio, where there's no visual element? It is said that a picture's worth a thousand words, and that seemed particularly true about trying to describe to a radio listener all the smells and sights of a garden in full growth. As I was to discover, it can take many graphic words and sounds to present the scene effectively, but it's a skill that develops with experience.

It took a while, about five or six days during which the family pestered me constantly, until I finally decided to get in touch with Jeremy. His original request for an allotment to adopt had sounded like a bit of a joke, so I thought I'd be equally light-hearted. I said I was perfectly willing to share my plot with him, that it was a great passion of mine, and that to me it was not just gardening but a whole way of life, with every visit a social occasion. I added that I thought there was this misconception that allotment gardening was hard work, but said it's never hard if you enjoy doing something and can mix the effort with the pleasures.

I explained that to me the allotment is a gym that helps keep me fit, it's my sunbed because it keeps me tanned, my stress counsellor because it's my way of relieving tension, and my means of relaxation in the open air.

I have all those benefits without paying large sums of money to join a club, and at the end of it I have the reward of taking home fresh, organic produce for my salad bowl or lunch plate. The place is so good for my health and well-being that anything I grow is an added bonus.

Well, I explained all this, not expecting anything to come from it.

Time passed and nothing happened: it turned out that being accepted for broadcasting is a long and involved procedure. About two weeks afterwards I came home at lunchtime on a mild, sunny April day, made myself a couple of sandwiches and a cup of coffee, and went outside to settle down on the patio. Just then the phone rang, and Anthea came out to say the BBC was on the line, for me. I didn't believe it, even when the caller announced she was 'Jessica from the BBC'.

'It's Keith Harris who put you up to this, isn't it? Where did he find you then, to get you to ring me up and pretend you're from the BBC?' I asked her.

'Oh no,' she said, 'this really is the BBC.'

'I reckon he's getting his own back for a practical joke I played on him a while ago,' I said. 'But go on. Now you've gone to all this trouble and he's obviously briefed you, I'll play along.'

I should explain that Keith is a very good friend of mine, someone I'd worked beside since the early 1970s. He's got a wicked sense of humour, rather like mine; our sons were a similar age and so our families went away on holiday together; and we both tended to take part in anything going,

3

usually winding each other up (and everyone else) wherever we were.

Now Keith had a habit of making a big thing of other people's birthdays, adorning the front of their house or garden, for example, with huge banners saying 'Give a hoot!' or 'Go and knock on the door!' So on his fiftieth birthday I thought I'd dress up as a town crier for a lark, and I managed to borrow the full ceremonial outfit from a real crier: big red coat, tails, shirt, dicky bow, hat and bell.

Then I went round the houses near where Keith lived, knocking on all the doors and asking if I could borrow the children to go along and serenade him. Up and down the streets I went, ringing my bell and looking like the Pied Piper with this long stream of children walking behind me. When we reached Keith's house I could see him with his family through the window, sitting down to a meal. All the children lined up behind me, and I produced my scroll and rang the bell as loud as I could, shouting, 'Oyez, oyez. Keith Harris is fifty today.' And then all the children burst into a chorus of 'Happy Birthday'.

I knew he would try to get his own back if he could, but when 'Jessica from the BBC' began to interview me it became obvious she really was who she said she was, and I had to apologize for my initial doubts. She went on to ask me a whole range of searching questions.

Later I found out there had been hundreds of applicants, and I wondered why they had picked me out of all the others. Jessica explained that she would ask each applicant to tell her about their allotment, and most people responded, 'What do you want to know?' But I had launched straight into describing my plot and my life on the allotments, which apparently showed the kind of enthusiasm they were looking for and an ability to think quickly. I obviously enjoyed talking about it, which she said stood me in good stead.

Again everything went quiet for two or three weeks. Then I had a call from Rebecca at the BBC, following up the conversation I'd had with Jessica. They were now down to a shortlist of allotments for Jeremy Vine's show, she said, and she wanted to ask a few more questions about mine. So we discussed the social life of the allotments, what was enjoyable about being there and what I did there besides actually gardening, how much time I spent there, and so on. And that was that.

Five weeks went by this time, with nothing more at all until Phil Jones called me on that memorable 1 July 2003. They were down to the last candidates by then and he was ringing each of us for a chat to help him decide who was going to join the show. He did his best to put me off.

'This is a live show,' he said, 'and there'll be no script. Jeremy will probably talk to you beforehand to get a feel for things, but he knows nothing about gardening and has a habit of going his own way, despite what he's been told. The listeners are there, you've got no chance to think, you just go straight in. Do you reckon you can cope with the uncertainty and actually talk live on radio like that?'

I told him I was pretty sure I could as I had addressed rooms full of people before as part of my job and I was used to thinking on my feet, so that didn't frighten me. And I appreciated there was nothing worse on live radio than silence.

It was then he said, 'Well, that sounds good to me. You're on on Friday!'

I had a few lingering reservations about the whole idea. I had just retired from a busy life in industry and was looking forward to working my allotment in peace and quiet. I didn't want the location of the site made public in a nationwide broadcast, potentially exposing the place to vandals or unwelcome publicity. And I still wasn't convinced in my own mind that radio was the best medium for talking about allotment life. But I kept all that to myself.

Little did I suspect then that the programme I was sure would be a one-off would lead to a fortnightly date with 'Terry's allotment in the Rhondda valley' for the next three years, something which still seems to me truly amazing.

The day of the first show duly came round. It was 4 July, Independence Day. Jeremy was hosting an hour-long special that Friday, with a gardening expert in the studio and me on the allotment on the end of my mobile. I felt rather nervous, naturally. Their usual practice is to ring about a quarter of an hour before the programme, and then you're stuck with the mobile to your ear, checking the sound is getting through all right and waiting for your cue.

At that point it really sank in that I had no script and no idea whatsoever of what was going to happen, what Jeremy would talk about or whether I would dry up. I knew there'd be this gardening expert in the studio for an hour with Jeremy, which presumably meant they would be sharing the entire hour with me based on the plot. And I thought, how on earth is this going to work?

Then I was cued in, and Jeremy started with 'We're going over to this allotment in the Rhondda now. What do you grow on this allotment then, Terry?'

I said, 'Well, I'll walk you through. I'm in the greenhouse at the moment, but I'll walk down the plot and explain to you what's growing here. In the greenhouse I've got tomatoes, cucumbers and peppers. Now we've come out into the open air and I'm walking round the corner, and the first thing I come to is a gooseberry bush. Then there's my courgettes, along the edge here are my strawberries, there's my parsnips, there are my carrots, there's my onions, and then I come to my Brussels sprouts. And now I'm coming to my cabbage . . .'

At that point he broke in and said, 'Just how big is this thing?'

'It's ten perch,' I said.

There was a stunned silence. Then the gardening expert asked, 'How big is ten perch?'

I added, 'That's ten perch in old money.'

'Yes, but how big *is* ten perch?'

Remember those maths tables we all used to chant at school? All about '30¼ square yards are 1 rod, pole or perch; 160 rods, poles or perches are 1 acre', and so on?

I said, 'Well, one perch is thirty and a quarter square yards (25 sq m), so that's 300 to 325 square yards (250 sq m) alto-gether. If you want to visualize it in the studio, it's about the size of an outdoor tennis court, just to give you a rough idea.'

'So how much *more* stuff have you got out there?'

I said, 'Well, I've got peas, I've got broad beans, I've got runner beans, I've got French beans, I've got shallots, I've got garlic, and I've got cauliflowers, broccoli . . .'

And they broke in again: 'Just how much *do* you grow?'

So I said, 'Well, everything that you'd go to buy fresh from the supermarket shelf, I tend to grow myself.'

That seemed to cut the ice and certainly settled me down, because once I'd started talking about my plot I was on familiar territory, and when that happens any nervousness tends to disappear.

It all seemed to be going well. There was a light-hearted humorous atmosphere, and later lots of listeners rang in with questions for us to answer. Somebody wanted to know about ideas for scaring off birds, and Jeremy asked me what I'd recommend.

'Well,' I said, 'I find the best thing to do, and it's very elementary, is to scrounge some old CDs and hang them up around the place. The noise and the glint of them tends to keep the birds off the crops. But it only works for a while.'

'Oh,' he said, 'any particular CDs?'

I said, 'Personally I find Des O'Connor works best!'

I was on for the full hour, and in some ways it felt a long time to spend on my mobile, always with the fear that it was going to let me down. I'd charged it up five times earlier that morning, just to be safe.

It worked a treat, though, and at the end of the show I had a text message from Jeremy, saying, 'Thanks very much, that seemed to go well, and we'll be in touch.' I thought maybe it was my comparative naivety about broadcasting that helped create the right atmosphere of spontaneity. I certainly never expected that programme to lead to a regular Friday afternoon appearance live on Radio 2.

Everybody I knew was tuned in to the programme. My friend Albie on the next plot had a battery radio in the greenhouse we all call his 'café', and many of the lads on the allotments were packed in there listening. Whenever I looked up across the path they would be there waving, and afterwards I had to take a lot of ribbing from friends when I went into my local pub. But it was fun, and I learned that in broadcasting the initial nervousness is something you really need to get you psyched up and the adrenalin flowing.

And before long I found that I was looking forward to doing the show live from Jeremy Vine's 'adopted allotment' on the side of our Welsh mountain, sharing with his five million or more listeners something I've always loved doing, ever since I started gardening there over fifty years ago.

Allotment becomes radio star

AN ALLOTMENT IN THE south Wales valleys is becoming one of the most famous plots in the UK after it was 'adopted' by the BBC's *Jeremy Vine Show*.

Terry Walton, 57, who has the allotment in Tonypandy in the Rhondda valley, has become a regular on the lunchtime programme talking about his garden. Every couple of weeks, Mr Walton is featured walking around the allotment and describing how things are growing.

Green-fingered Mr Walton offered up his gardening patch after hearing an appeal from Jeremy Vine to 'adopt an allotment'.

'Everyone up here gathers around the radio and listens when I'm on air and we have a great laugh and joke about it all,' said Mr Walton. 'I have had a lot of people taking the mickey out of me when I go down the pub, but it's all in good humour. I definitely recommend gardening to anyone – it is great and although it takes a bit of patience you will soon see the results of your work. I'm retired now, but when I was working I often used to come up here at the end of a hard day, and after an hour of digging I'd be relaxed again. I know that *EastEnders'* Arthur Fowler had quite a famous allotment in the soap, but I think that mine is becoming almost as famous,' he laughed.

Jeremy Vine explained how the allotment feature started: 'It all came about after we did a one-hour special on allotments and we got more responses from that than any other subject including Iraq. We realized that there were a whole lot of people who were totally engrossed in their allotments. As we do a lot of serious issues on the show, we realized we needed to have something more stress-busting, and we decided to adopt an allotment. We had about 150 offers from people and we had to go through them very carefully, but Terry's allotment is absolutely perfect and he is a real character himself.'

Source: BBC NEWS:
http://news.bbc.co.uk/go/pr/fr/-/1/hi/wales/south_east/3107971.stm
Published: 2003/07/30 15:04:58 GMT © BBC MMVI

CHAPTER ONE

A Closely Knit Community

I WAS BORN in the Rhondda valley, just five miles away from my present house in the Ely valley, so I've lived and gardened in the Welsh valleys all my life. What we in these parts know as 'the valleys' are a collection of south Wales communities that sprang up along a number of almost parallel rivers, all flowing in deep gashes down the hillside and draining the enormous quantities of rainfall off the Black Mountains and Brecon Beacons away southwards down to the sea.

The valley of the river Rhondda is perhaps the best known of all. 'The Rhondda', as it is generally called, actually consists of two parallel valleys, which meet at a town called Porth (Welsh for 'gateway') and are fondly known as the Rhondda Fach (from the word *bach*, meaning 'small') and the Rhondda

Fawr (from *mawr*, or 'big'). Both valleys are steep-sided, with the rivers running through right at the bottom.

The coal mines that were the life blood of the communities tended to be at the base of the valleys, while houses for the people who worked in them were built on the slopes. These houses were laid out in neat terraces, row upon row of them lining the hillsides and often flanking very narrow streets. At least the mine owners had the forethought to provide each of these closely packed houses with a large back garden. This allowed miners to enjoy valuable and reviving leisure time outdoors at the end of a working day spent in dark, dusty conditions below ground. The garden was a place to relax and recover after a hard shift at the coalface, to see the sun and sky, and to enjoy the fresh air while growing their own wholesome vegetables to feed the family.

Every mine built its own rows of houses, each group forming a little township servicing the pit. Although a stranger to the area might not recognize any clearly defined boundaries as one community merges imperceptibly into the next, these townships were all separately named and had their own strong identities. People were proud to state where they lived, and you can still hear this loyalty to a particular community today when local football or rugby teams play each other, or one choir competes against another.

Working conditions down the mines were dangerous, and several major tragedies blackened the history of the area when explosions and roof falls killed sometimes hundreds of men and boys. The men worked in appalling conditions for long periods and therefore spent most of their lives together.

Far below the surface, with just candles for illumination, they depended totally on one another for their safety, often for their lives, and this bred strong bonds of friendship and a well-developed, utterly local sense of humour that enabled them to endure the harsh conditions. This distinctive sense of fun remains today in the people who live in the close-knit communities of the valleys, long after all the pits closed and the hillsides turned green once more.

Inevitably the people who grew up and lived together in the valleys also had a great tradition of cooperation outside work. All the people who lived around us when I was a child had very little money, but they were always willing to help anybody in difficulties in any way they could. When everyone experienced the same working conditions and lifestyle, sharing was bred into you from an early age.

You find this on the allotments, which are almost a minia-ture version of the local community. If anyone is struggling with an overgrown plot or has a crop failure or cannot tend the plot because of illness, others rally round to help out. They might provide physical assistance, offer to share produce or plants, or simply water and ventilate the greenhouse until the plotholder is fit and well. It's the same today as it has been throughout my lifetime.

The valleys built up a reputation for exporting high-quality coal, a vital trade that sustained the area, making landowners wealthy and guaranteeing the workers a living, and eventually shot it to prominence in the 1920s during the years of indus-trial unrest. The miners' strike of 1926 demonstrated the loyalty and solidarity of the valley people, who remained steadfast through those dreadful times. For more than a week Britain was virtually paralysed when many workers came out to support the miners in their dispute with the government over proposals for change in the coal industry. After nine days the Trades Union Congress accepted better terms and recom-mended a return to work.

The miners, however, rejected the deal and were duly locked out of the pits, but after a long and acrimonious dispute they were forced to choose between starving or returning to work under much less favourable conditions. Many survived only thanks to the produce everyone grew in gardens and allotments. It was the suffering and injustice of those bitter times that welded together a community of people who cared for and helped each other in a period of extreme hardship, forging a solidarity that still exists today.

The area had already achieved notoriety in 1910 when Winston Churchill, then Home Secretary, sent in troops to quell disturbances. Striking miners at the Cambrian group of pits were picketing the power house at Glamorgan Colliery, just down the road in Llwynypia. This engine house was vital for keeping the colliery open because it provided the power for pumps that kept the pit from flooding. When things turned ugly, the police baton-charged the crowd, splitting them into two groups, one of which rampaged through Tonypandy, smashing and looting the shops in the main street. Fearing they were losing control, local officials appealed to Churchill to send troops to help stabilize the volatile situation.

This is a chapter of Rhondda history that has become enshrined in valley folklore. It's often said that the men were the strong participants in this drama, but stories I've been told show it was the women who maintained the solidarity during those testing times. They met in groups and organized the soup kitchens which kept youngsters fed and prevented the men from starving, often while going without themselves. Throughout the bitter dispute they supported their menfolk, who at times must have been desperate and frustrated that no end to the long confrontation was in sight. Even now men think they are the strength in the valleys, but don't you believe it: it's the women who keep the community alive, along with many of the traditional family values.

Even today there's a strange sense of belonging in valley life which remains with you wherever you go in the world. You can recognize a valley person anywhere: someone marked out by a strong sense of fun, willing to share their last penny with you, dependable in a crisis and loyal to the end. (The fact that I have no sense of humour whatsoever and must be the tightest-fisted Welshman around doesn't prevent me from being a true valley boy!)

Surrounded by these traditional values, I grew up in a typical Rhondda mining house. Most homes built by the mine owners for their workers were made of locally quarried stone. Due to the size of mining families, which usually consisted of two, often three generations all living under the same roof, most houses had three or four bedrooms (ours had four).

In many houses family life centred on the kitchen and living room; the front room was the 'best' room, reserved for special occasions. We were only allowed in this hallowed place after bath night and dressed in our Sunday best. When great-aunts came visiting they were shown into the front room and then we were ushered in to greet them like royalty, very politely although not quite with a bow. The upside was that cake would always be served, which made up for the pomp and ceremony we had to endure.

As was usual in those days we had no bathroom. Bath night involved setting out an old tin bath in front of the coal fire and filling it with hot water that had been boiled on the fire – there was no hot running water then, and certainly no central heating. Once the ritual filling of the bath was completed the whole family would use it in a set order: children usually went first so they could go off to bed afterwards, with father next and finally mother. Then followed the long and laborious task of emptying this bath of water, which had to be baled out with an old bucket until it was light enough to carry out to the back yard, where the rest could be poured away. When it wasn't in use, the bath hung on the wall in the back garden, and my childhood memories are punctuated by the sound of the family bath banging noisily in the wind.

There were two kinds of bath then: the bungalow bath, which was long with a smooth bottom, and the more basic round or oval bath embossed with uncomfortable circular ribs for strength. Even less comfortable were the repairs that came with age. Eventually the bath would begin to leak, and when this happened you would buy from the ironmonger's a couple of big steel washers. These were arranged inside and outside the hole with two rubber pads in between and a big bolt going through from one side to the other. Then you'd tighten it all down until the rubber sealed the hole in the bath. The trouble was that when you sat in the bath this bolt would be sticking through, and to sit down safely meant packing a flannel round the end of the bolt. That was all right until you had four or five bolts poking through the bottom, and then you'd have to change the bath. It wouldn't have been so bad if the bolt heads were on the inside, but that never happened: you always had to sit on the sharp ends.

All the same, I fondly remember the cosy glow of bathing in front of a roaring coal fire in the winter months, although there was also a certain amount of danger involved. The side of the bath closest to the fire would heat up as time went on, and if you were not careful you could easily burn your bum on the hot metal. You had to beware of flying hot cinders, too!

Like everybody else, we had no indoor toilet. Ours was next to the coal shed, and we had to cross the yard and go down the garden to reach it. Our back yard was a dark, dingy place because the garden was dug into the mountainside, which was held back by a wall fifteen feet (4½ m) high, with numerous steps to get to it. Not surprisingly, the back yard, with its strange shadows, seemed a frightening place at night and not much better by day, thanks to this high wall: only plants with a taste for gloom could survive there.

There was no light in the toilet, only the candle you took with you, hoping all the time it didn't blow out before you could get back indoors. Nor was there any soft, quilted toilet tissue in those days. We used old newspapers torn into squares and made into a pad that was hung behind the toilet door on a wire threaded through a hole in the corner. As a youngster I always found it frustrating when I'd rip off a piece of this newspaper and start to read the story on it, only to find the exciting bit was on another piece that had already been used.

The house was a little crowded at times, with my mother, father, brother and eventually me as well as my aunt, uncle and cousin. Relatives living together in the same house was quite usual, especially since the last child to marry normally stayed at home to look after the parents and raise a family there. But we were sharing for a slightly different reason: my parents and brother had come to the Rhondda after a wartime bomb wiped out their home in Coventry and forced them to move in with the only relatives who could accommodate them quickly.

We might have been cramped, but living together did have its pleasures, especially around Christmas time because my brother's birthday was on Christmas Day, my aunt's on Boxing Day, my cousin's on New Year's Day and my own three days later. With four of the seven people living in our household celebrating birthdays so close together at that special time of year, the festive season was always enormous fun.

For my mother the Rhondda was home. My father came from Ramsgate, in Kent, where Mother had been sent when she was a fourteen-year-old girl, along with her sister Gaytha, to work 'in service' at his parents' boarding house. It was common practice in the early part of the twentieth century for daughters of poorer households to go into service when they reached their early teens. There was no further education for them in those days, and all children were expected to contribute to the family income as soon as they could.

Sons generally stayed at home and followed their fathers down the pits, but there was little work locally for girls and so they would be sent anywhere in Britain to work as cleaners, maids and general servants in large houses where domestic help was needed. They would then send home part of their meagre wages to boost the family budget. It was not an easy life: they worked long hours, had few privileges and rarely saw their families. But it turned out well for my mother because it was in Ramsgate that she met my father and got married.

I don't tend to waste much time on regrets, but I do wish (now it's too late) that I had asked my parents more about themselves. I was brought up in an era when parents never talked about life before you were on the scene, and if you didn't enquire you weren't told. I never met most of my mother's or father's brothers or sisters, and with the passage of time all my parents' early life is lost to me. We were not inquisitive about these things, which is a pity: few of us realize early in life just how important family history can become once the connections with the past are gone. It would be nice to think my parents had a romantic meeting and an exciting courtship, but all that will now remain a mystery to me for ever.

What I do know is that my parents married in the 1930s and settled in Ramsgate, where my brother Eric was born.

18

They stayed there until just after the start of the Second World War, when they moved to the Radford area of Coventry to be closer to my mother's family, who had moved there to find work in the car industry.

Here in the Rhondda there was coal mining and little else. My mother's family had worked down the mines but wanted something better, so they decided, like many others, that the best way out was to move to the Midlands, which were becoming quite prosperous as the engineering industry developed. After joining them there my mother started to work in the munitions industry and my father found a job in a factory.

One evening the sirens announced another air raid on Coventry, which was targeted because there was a lot of heavy engineering and many ammunition factories. The air-raid shelter was at the end of the street where my family lived, and they duly trooped down there to sit out the raid. After the all-clear sounded they found that the whole block of houses where they lived had been flattened and the remains of a German aircraft were sticking out of the wreckage. They had nothing left but the clothes they stood up in. For safety, they all headed back to the valleys, to live with my aunt, uncle and cousin in the house where, in 1946, I was born.

So ultimately it was thanks to Mr Hitler that my long love affair with my allotment on the hillside developed, and maybe it was the fresh mountain air of the Rhondda which ensured there was a Terry Walton in the first place!

My earliest memories begin in the fifties, when the Rhondda was still dominated by the mining industry and almost every village had its own pit, employing the majority of local men. This was not the only employment in the valleys: there were also several engineering companies, such as Bramber Springs, which made components for the motor industry, T. C. Jones, making structural steel for buildings, and Rollo Hardy, who produced steel tubing. But most men worked in the pits, father and son alike.

There were no pithead baths in those days, and men coming up from a shift underground walked home in their grimy clothes, their faces still covered with coal dust. I can see them now, with black faces and gleaming white teeth, and typically carrying a metal food box under one arm and a few blocks of wood from pit props under the other for the coal fire that would be blazing brightly at home. Their wives would have the tin bath full of hot water in front of the fire, ready for them to wash as they walked into the house. I reckon the drains and sewers of the Rhondda must have enough small coal down them to keep a power station going for years.

The role of a woman in the mining communities was clearly established: she was there to keep house, bring up the children and prepare a meal for the man returning from work. No women worked outside the home in those days, but that's not to say they didn't have to work hard.

There were none of the modern appliances then to help keep the house clean. With no vacuum cleaners, floors were swept with a broom and corners with a brush and dustpan. The menfolk's grimy clothes were all washed by hand, using a scrubbing board and the tin bath. Ironing was a particular chore, with a large, chunky flat-iron constantly needing to be reheated over the open fire. Thank God for technology!

Microwave ovens, ready-made meals and pre-packaged food didn't exist then. Everything was freshly cooked, with produce grown on the allotment or in the back garden, or bought from the local shop that stood in every street. My mother spent much of her time making hot dinners, invariably consisting of meat, vegetables, and gravy made with the meat stock and water from the veg.

During the long cold winters she would buy lambs' breasts, which she diced and then put in a large pot. To this she would add plenty of water and whatever vegetables my father had growing on his plot or in store: parsnips, swedes, potatoes, onions. This pot of goodies would simmer for hours on the open fire and become *cawl* (traditional Welsh broth), which was consumed over several days, getting richer and tastier as each day passed, and helping to keep out the cold. By contrast, summer meant plenty of salads, predominantly lettuce, new potatoes and home-cooked boiled ham. It's no wonder that allotments thrived in the valley in those days because they were the major source of all this fresh food.

In retrospect, life was hard and basic, although relatively comfortable compared to what my mother must have experienced during the twenties, living away from home in one tiny room in a strange place and working long hours for a very small wage, most of which was sent home. But my childhood days were happy because we felt safe. While the collieries were king and provided employment, there was a clear distinction between the roles of men, whose strong, proud tradition was to provide for the family, and women, who were there to keep the home going. And I think families on the whole felt content with that arrangement.

Mothers would take small children to school and the older ones would walk on their own – the roads were safe and the maximum distance would be three-quarters of a mile to a mile each way, which you did all the year round. And when you came home your mother was there. There were no latch-key kids, you didn't come in and have to wait long for anything, and you would always sit down together as a family for a meal.

You could trust people then, and felt secure. Nobody in the street had any more wealth than anyone else, so there was no cause for jealousy between neighbours, and this was something that helped cement the community together. No doors were ever locked, and neighbours would frequently walk into each other's houses.

The money to pay the milkman would be left outside the door with a note and no one else would ever touch it. When I was a child our milk was delivered by horse and cart, and you were lucky if the milkman's horse left a pile of manure outside your door, as this was a much sought-after prize for feeding the rhubarb that grew in everybody's back garden. Sometimes it wasn't clear whose door had been favoured, and then rival claims to the manure might cause an argument.

To think this manure went on to the very rhubarb that we children would be given instead of sweets! Sweets were always in short supply and we received them only on special occasions such as Christmas. Instead my mother used to cut short sticks of rhubarb from the garden and give them to me with a paper bag containing some sugar. I simply dipped the raw rhubarb sticks in the sugar and ate them. It was that or nothing.

One of the most vivid memories I have of my childhood in the early fifties is of the empty streets completedly devoid of cars. The only vehicles you would encounter were double-decker buses and the odd car, usually large and always black, belonging to a doctor or maybe a schoolteacher. Those empty streets made great playgrounds for us children, and it's sad to see how congested the valley roads are today.

We had no expensive toys to play with, but we were early experts at adapting or recycling common household objects. Hours of fun could be derived from an old tin can or from two pieces of stick, one long and the other short and stubby, that were used in a game we called 'cat 'n' doggy'. The object was to tap the short piece of stick with the long piece to make it jump in the air; then, while it was still airborne, you had to whack it with the long piece. The winner was the one who sent it the furthest distance.

If you were really lucky you might own a *gambo*, a cart made by your father from odd pieces of wood, with old pram wheels at the front and rear. The plank bearing the front wheels was joined to the main body with a bolt and a piece of string was attached at each end for steering. Most streets in the valleys sloped dramatically and there was no danger from cars, so you could safely hurtle downhill on this contraption at alarming speeds. It had no brakes, of course.

By today's standards there wasn't what you'd call plenty of things for children to do, though. There was an old tip nearby where we used to kick a football around. A boy with Down's syndrome lived at the little village shop in our street, but we looked after him because he had a real leather football. His mother would ask if he could play with us, he'd bring his football and we'd all go off and play together up the tip, making sure he was fully involved, otherwise he'd go home and take his football with him. It suited him and his mother because he was playing with other children, and no one else we knew had a leather football. Sometimes we would even get a handful of sweets from his mother's shop as well.

Often we simply armed ourselves with a pack of jam sandwiches and a bottle of pop, and headed up the beautiful mountainsides surrounding our homes. There we would slide down the grassy slopes using part of an old cardboard box as a home-made sleigh, which would amuse us for hours until it fell apart. (It amazes me that, despite the sledging practice we all had as children, no Welsh team has ever won an Olympic gold in the bobsleigh event!) Then it was time to go home.

'Home' in the fifties was a close-knit community with a strict code of behaviour: authority was respected, and there was no wanton vandalism and no one was terrorized. If a teacher gave you a 'clip round the ear' (something that wouldn't be allowed today), you'd never go home and tell your father because he would discipline you too. I cannot recall my father ever raising a hand to me – but then, as he was a six-foot three-inch giant, just one word was enough to bring me back into line.

I remember as a seven-year-old playing with my friends on Partridge Square, where there was a large bus station and another building with a wide roof. We decided to shin up the drainpipe to sit on the roof. We were all sitting there like a row of rooftop statues when along came Sergeant Jones, the local constable. He wanted to know what we thought we were doing up there, and told us to get down immediately, which we all did sheepishly. The sergeant gave us a stern lecture and took us home to our parents. There was no sympathy there, only another severe talking-to and a ban from playing outdoors for several days.

When I was still small and wandering about the allotments one day, I spotted a bush of blackcurrants, heavily loaded with juicy fruit, on Alf Daniel's plot. Now Alf was a stern, military kind of guy who didn't stand any nonsense. I looked round furtively but couldn't see anyone about, so I walked slowly over to the bush. Hardly had I grabbed a handful of juicy currants when there was a loud shout from behind the row of runner beans. 'Oi!' the voice roared. It was Alf, of course, scaring me witless. And not only did he frighten the life out of me by his sudden appearance: he took me over to my father, who told me off in no uncertain terms and banned me from the allotments for two weeks. That fortnight seemed like for ever to me, and it was a devastating blow to be forbidden my daily foray to my father's plot to see how my crops were doing. Harsh punishment indeed!

First allotment memories

I WAS VERY YOUNG, maybe three or four. My mother had dressed me in short trousers, a short-sleeved shirt and black wellies (my customary footwear ever since). Holding my father's hand very tightly I entered this new world through a large set of gates, and I can still hear the loud, metallic clang as my father pulled them back to let us through.

I stared in wonder as we walked along the neatly manicured grass paths, through vast areas of lush green foliage punctuated here and there by splashes of coloured flowers. We walked for what seemed ages, with strange voices calling out as we passed, 'Going gardening with your daddy then, are you?'

Eventually we reached a plot with a small shed in the corner and a little stone step, where my father sat me down while he walked out into the green rows and began pulling out the little plants growing there. I didn't understand at the time that he was weeding his plot.

I sat watching him intently as he moved along the rows, putting these green things in a small bucket he carried. All the while he was working he kept →

looking up and talking to me. Finally he came back to the shed to fetch a long stick with a strange metal hook on the end (a swan-necked hoe, as I discovered later). He dragged this up and down the weeded rows, breaking up the earth he had trodden flat.

That experience probably started my interest in gardening. Many more visits followed, each one adding to my fascination and enjoyment, until at last he allowed me to join in and I was hooked for life. There was one particular day when it had just rained after a long dry spell, and the air had that earthy, pungent smell of dampness that lodges in your nostrils. Even now visiting my plot in the same conditions vividly rekindles all those early times on the allotment with my dad.

We seldom went away on holiday, and if we did it was usually to a relative. Because some of the family were still living in Coventry, the Welsh contingent would often travel up there together on the train two days before Christmas, coming back some time before the New Year. To me at that early age it seemed an extraordinary expedition. I remember overcrowded trains leaving Cardiff station, all packed with families reuniting for the festive season.

When we finally arrived after a six-hour journey at my grandparents' home in Coventry, we would find the house festooned with home-made decorations. Waking up on Christmas morning to a stocking stuffed with goodies – choco-lates and fresh fruit such as apples and tangerines – was a taste of what paradise must be like. No expensive presents, of course, but a simple wooden toy or a couple of Dinky cars were enough to cause great excitement. After opening the presents we'd settle down to a mid-afternoon feast of a Christmas dinner.

Sometimes in the summer we went to stay in Norfolk, where my father's sister lived: they had a farm, so if we went up there it was for a working holiday. If the Christmas journey to Coventry meant an expedition, venturing all the way to Norfolk was the ultimate adventure to me in my pre-teen years. We'd set off from Llwynypia station early in the morning, and after three changes of train and a whole day of travelling we would arrive exhausted at the little village of Watlington in Norfolk.

My uncle Frank grew sugar beet and wheat on his farm, and my first experience of driving a motorized vehicle came at the tender age of ten, when I was allowed to drive his tractor. In addition to being a farmer he was the local milkman, so while we were there we would be up at the crack of dawn to help out on the milk round. On our return to the farm (and before we could have breakfast) we had to collect all the eggs from the large sheds where he kept his chickens.

One of Frank's more obscure occupations was that of gravedigger for the local church. I well remember helping him and being somewhat bemused at the large hole we were digging in that picturesque churchyard. But the practice stood me in good stead and I became the best on the allotments at digging runner bean trenches, which I've always reckoned look like medieval burial mounds.

All that work, yet I was supposed to be on holiday and having a break from my allotment duties. But they do say hard work never did anyone any harm!

We weren't all that far from the sea where we lived in the

Rhondda, barely fifteen miles, but we had no easy means of getting there. We had no car and we never went on a bus, except for organized Sunday School outings. We would take a penny to Sunday School every week and that would pay for us children to go away for the day. All the children went to Sunday School because you could be sure of two trips a year, to places like Barry or Porthcawl.

One year we went to Aberavon, and that meant going on a steam train through a tunnel at the top of the valley. This tunnel started at the head of the Rhondda Fawr at Blaenrhondda and emerged several miles away on the other side of the mountain at Port Talbot. The train would be gently sauntering up the valley and then suddenly it would disappear into this dark chasm in the hillside. The lights only dimly lit the carriages, and children standing at the open windows would rush back to their seats to be with their parents in what seemed a dark hell-hole. With the windows all open the carriage would quickly fill with the distinctive smells of steam, sulphur and smoke trapped in the tunnel, leaving indelible impressions on young minds.

Mothers of children with chest complaints would make them stand at the open windows and breathe in this strong concoction of fumes, in the belief that the mixture would alleviate their symptoms. When we all emerged into the sunlight once more at the Port Talbot end of the tunnel, the pale faces of those poor children were covered with black spots like some dreadful disease, the result of the smuts being belched from the funnel of this steam monster. Port Talbot might have been only a few miles from home, but to us youngsters it meant an infernal trip to the other side of the world.

In the summer we went to the sea on double-decker buses, which would be packed with children because the church congregation in those days was enormous. Not that we kids were particularly religious: we all attended Sunday School and even enjoyed it, but really it was these trips every year that we went for.

Sometimes we visited Coney Beach, near Porthcawl, where they had a funfair. We were allowed a fixed sum of money for the fair, and when the money was gone, it was gone. So we'd spend all day on the beach, with our egg sandwiches and jam sandwiches (full of sand) and a bottle of pop. Then, just before we went home on the bus, we were allowed about an hour at the fair with our ten pence (4p), which seemed to last no time at all. And then it was all over.

Looking back at photographs of when I was a child, I'm amazed that when we went to the seaside we were dressed up exactly as if going to normal Sunday School. All the boys wore a shirt and tie, cap, short trousers, a pair of socks up to the knees and clean shoes. And we were expected to sit there and not get dirty. If I was allowed to go in the sea I had to wear 'bathers' – shaped like shorts – knitted by my mother. They were uncomfortable and seemed to stretch for miles in the water and fill up with sand, so that as you walked back up the beach these heavy wet woollen things would drag at you like a ton weight.

When I look back, childhood summers seem to have always been sunny. The sun can't have shone all the time, but you don't remember the wet days. When we had Double Summer Time (an economy measure to make the most of daylight by putting the clocks forward two hours) it seemed to be light sometimes until eleven o'clock at night, and bedtime didn't go down well with me. I'd complain bitterly at having to come in while the sun was still brightly shining. And then, after we children had gone to bed, all the women would take kitchen chairs outside, form a group on the pavement and knit. And you'd be stuck there, trying to sleep, with them all talking away and clacking their knitting needles.

Even though everybody else was the same, I remember being well aware that we were poor. Most of the time I lived in wellington boots. They appear in all the photographs of me as a child – I'd have a pair of short trousers on, a jumper about nine sizes too big, and always these wellingtons. And as they wore out, so my socks came into view at the toe.

You made your own fun as a family, because there was no television to sit down in front of, not until way into the sixties. For entertainment most people would congregate in the rarely used front room and play cards. Outside the home there was no bingo, and the church hall was the main focal point for entertainment: there they'd put on concerts, whist drives and other social events, and at Christmas there'd be a pantomime.

Everywhere in the valleys the church or chapel – mostly Anglican, but Methodist and Baptist too – was the centre of the community, together with the pubs, of course. But Sundays in Wales were 'dry' for a very long time, with all the pubs closed, and in some places it was well into the eighties before pubs could open on a Sunday. In Tenby, for example, you simply couldn't get an alcoholic drink on a Sunday unless you were a member of the Conservative Club.

It always seemed strange to me that there were so many Conservative clubs dotted round the valley, which has always been a staunch Labour stronghold. But as well as providing alcohol, the 'Con Clubs', as they were affectionately known, always had the best snooker tables and were run by efficient committees. I became a member of the Tonypandy Con Club and, like everyone else, had to go before the committee and swear allegiance to the Conservative Party. Few members were true to their vows, I'm certain, and it was always a bit of a joke at elections when the Conservative candidate actually gained fewer votes than there were club members. What people will do for a drink on a dry Sunday!

It was mainly the men who would go out for a drink, although I don't remember my father going very often to a pub or club. I think he was happier up on his allotment, which was probably entertainment enough for him. He had taken on a plot in the early forties, immediately after coming to the Rhondda from the Midlands, and as early as 1950 I would be there with him.

He'd often go up there for the whole day, with a couple of sandwiches and a flip-top Corona pop bottle that my mother filled with tea. My father thought nothing of drinking cold tea, something I couldn't stand. I would go up there with him and he would amuse me as long as he could until I'd had enough, when I would go back home – our house was only about a hundred yards away. As I got older I would stay longer and longer, until I was eleven and thought, I can do this. Before that I was simply sent or taken to the plot to be useful. Every family member was expected to help with the chores: you might run errands to the shop for your mother or help around the house. In my case I was usually expected to help my father on his allotment.

Terry's Tip for January

JANUARY IS THE TIME to carry out all your cleaning and maintenance jobs on the plot: as my father always insisted, an hour spent now is worth five in the spring when all your effort is needed to plant out your plot, and I've proved him right.

On a cold day, clean up the greenhouse to get rid of algae and pests lying in wait for the new season. I mix one capful of household bleach in half a bucket of warm water (or you can substitute a bleach-free alternative cleanser), and use this to wash all the frames and glass panes with a soft brush, making sure I brush well into all the nooks and crannies to kill any over-wintering pests lurking there. The clean glass will help to increase the amount of light in the greenhouse, which will stimulate the plants to grow more vigorously.

At the beginning of the growing season in February, while the days are still short and often grey, seedlings need as much light as they can get to give them a good start in life. This thorough clean-through before you re-erect staging and get everything set up for the earliest sowings is the best possible preparation for the new growing season.

Anthea's Recipe for January

Beetroot Jelly

IF YOU HAVE some beet in store in January, use a few roots for this recipe while they're still in good condition: the result will be a thick, pleasantly tart jelly that goes well with your cold meat dishes. These quantities will fill 2–3 1 lb (450 g) jars.

* 1 lb (450 g) beetroot
* 1 pint (600 ml) malt vinegar
* 4 oz (125 g) sugar
* 1 oz (25 g) powdered gelatine, plus water to mix

Boil the beetroot until tender; allow it to cool, then peel and dice into small cubes. Pack these loosely into jars.

Boil the vinegar and sugar together. Dissolve the gelatine in a little water, and then add this to the boiled vinegar.

Return to heat, bring slowly back to the boil, and then allow to cool.

Pour this liquor over the beetroot in the jars, getting out as much air as possible.

Seal the jars with clingfilm, and when cold fit their lids. Once opened, store in the fridge.

CHAPTER TWO

A Plot on the Mountain

THE ALLOTMENTS WHERE my father had his plot, and where I garden to this day, lie on a steep slope near the foot of the mountain, Mynydd Tyntyla. This location has always influenced the way the plots are worked as well as the things I used to do there as a child.

If you live anywhere in a Welsh valley it is very difficult to avoid the effects of geography. The river, main roads and railway all tend to run side by side in a ribbon at the bottom while the terraced houses creep up the lower slopes on either flank, so whenever you leave your house you have to climb or drop down a hillside.

Coal mines occur both in those valley bottoms and on the hillsides, while the tops are generally the preserve of windswept farms and their flocks of hardy mountain sheep.

Our bit of the Rhondda valley, with its townships of Tonypandy, Trealaw, Llwynypia and Porth, was typical in that the work of most men there was firmly based on mining, although there were a few other occupations, including plenty of building. My father worked a concrete mixer.

We had one of the very first soft drinks companies, Thomas & Evans, later famous throughout the land as the manufacturer of Corona soft drinks. William Evans originally set himself up in Porth as a grocer in 1888, and in 1903 he started a business bottling mineral water. By the early twenties (helped considerably by the temperance movement) his sales were strong enough for him to form a private limited company producing Corona soft drinks. Although the firm is no longer based in Porth, the original industrial premises remain as the Pop Factory, a studio where they make television programmes and hold concerts.

The various soft drinks they produced were basically water, flavouring and a colouring, together with the carbon dioxide that put the bubbles in – their advertising slogan was 'Every bubble's passed its FIZZical'. This carbon dioxide was added not as gas but frozen, as 'dry ice', which was made at a small works near the allotment site. As we walked to school we'd pass the place and see all these blocks of dry ice outside, waiting to be taken to the bottling works at Porth, and we used to snip bits off to throw at each other.

To keep the drinks pressurized, the bottles had a rubber ring at the neck and a movable bit of steel wire to clip the top in place. All these bottles were returnable and carried a deposit – no broken glass littering the streets in those days, bottles were too valuable – so we'd collect them up and take them back to the shop to earn a few pennies to spend on sweets.

Popular sweets then were huge round gobstoppers that

kept you quiet for some time; Spangles, which were long packets of square fruit sweets; and Lossindant mints, hard stripy humbugs. My own favourite was the sherbet dab or dip, a lollipop in a bag of white powder flavoured with lemon juice: you licked the lollipop, dipped it in the sherbet and then sucked off the tart flavour – yum. I suspect you might have a problem walking through the valleys these days carrying a packet of a fine white substance!

Most men living around us worked down one of the pits as coal miners or 'colliers'. The last bus to come down the valley was always called the colliers' bus, because it would be full of miners coming off the late shift.

There were two kinds of coal mine in the valley, deep pits and levels, neither of them pleasant to work in. In the deep pits you needed a mineshaft and a cage to reach the workface. These pits had a vertical shaft that went down a long way because the best coal, which was high-quality anthracite, was very deep, far below the valley bottom. The principal pits near where we lived were the Glamorgan or 'Scotch' Colliery, which closed the year before I was born, and the Lewis Merthyr and Great Western mines, which merged to become Tymawr Colliery when I was about twelve.

An unfortunate result of the deep pit workings was the amount of waste material that came up with the coal from the underground shafts. This waste, popularly called 'slag', needed to be disposed of somewhere, and the cheapest method was simply to dump it on the beautiful hillsides, where it formed unnatural black and misshapen hills that deeply scarred the once wooded and green valley sides for decades.

Fortunately nature, with a little help from enlightened people after the closure of the pits, has reclaimed the hillsides – albeit in their new artificial form – and restored them to their former glory. So to an unknowing eye the valleys look green and natural again, already adorned by large densely wooded areas of great beauty, filled with deciduous trees such as oak, ash, a large scattering of white-barked silver birch, and rowans that speckle the hillsides with their bright clusters of red berries as summer draws on. Gone are the days when the hills were cloaked in drab forests of firs, grown to serve the insatiable appetite of the mines for pit props.

In addition to the deep pits there were 'levels', horizontal mines that you simply walked into. They were driven into the face of the mountain as far as you needed to go to get the coal, which was dug and brought out in 'drams', solid trucks that were pushed out manually along the level because there was no mechanized means of bringing them out. This coal from the levels was steam coal, quite inferior to the anthracite used for making steel and exported all over the world from Cardiff docks.

Coal was everywhere when I was kid. Colliers were entitled to a supply of concessionary coal, about six or seven loads a year delivered to the front door in a big two- or three-ton tipper truck. This would be divided into separate compartments, one for each address, so the truck would arrive at one house, open up the first compartment and tip the load, leaving it there at the roadside in front of your house before moving on to the next drop-off. And this ton of coal was exactly as mined, in huge chunks mixed with loads of 'small coal'.

If you weren't a miner you bought in supplies that were broken down into nuggets and bagged and delivered by a coal merchant, who would take it through to your coal house or the coal *cwtch* as it was known, situated in the back yard. Fortunately in our house there were no fancy carpets on the floor because when our coal was delivered, the bags of black nuggets had to be carried through two rooms to reach the back yard.

The Coal Board, on the other hand, delivered and tipped it loose, and it was the householder's job then to carry those big lumps indoors. Alternatively you traded your 'small coal' with someone in the street who didn't have a concessionary supply: they would carry and stack your delivery for you and in exchange would take all the small stuff home in buckets, and this was used to cover the merchant's coal when banking up the fire at night to keep it in until the next day. *And* you'd get the street in front of the house swept up for you as well.

Cwtch

THIS VERSATILE WORD is widely used in the valleys and beyond, even by those whose first language is English. The '*w*' is a vowel, sounding rather like a short English 'oo', and the whole word rhymes with 'Dutch', spoken with a North Country accent. It has a number of uses:

- The basic meaning, linked to the similar word *cwt* ('hut' or 'den'), is the shed or space where coal was kept.
- It's also a cuddle, as in 'Give us a *cwtch* then', used particularly where children are involved.
- Therapists use the term to mean a healthy hug to keep the spirits up – even the Lions rugby team have *cwtch* sessions!
- It's commonly used to order a noisy or disobedient dog to its corner: 'Bad boy, go *cwtch*!' →

- It can mean to hide something: 'Keep that safely *cwtched*, now.'
- You'll find *cwtch* bars in pubs and restaurants, cosy corners that were once called 'snugs'.
- And children use it in play to keep others away: 'Stay out of my *cwtch!*'

There were two distinct levels at the rear of our allotments, little private mines where individuals worked. There were a lot of small levels like that in the valley, started by people who knew the coal was there and simply went up and dug it out. You'd reach the coal very quickly; not the decent seams for which you had to go well in but certainly enough to run a domestic fire. All you had to do was come to some arrangement with the landowner about mineral rights, probably paying him a percentage of whatever you made from the mine. There are still remnants of those workings up on the mountain above us today, although there's no trace of the levels themselves, only the water that runs from them and supplies all our allotment plots.

It was the construction of a new level on the mountainside which ended my father's brief venture into farming in the fifties. Next to the allotments were three acres of ground, known as Cae Cae Farm, that somehow became available, and my father decided to take it on as a smallholding, with pigs – two huge sows, I remember, quite enormous animals – ducks and a lot of chickens. Whenever one of these had a clutch of chicks, they were brought into our front room and kept in a box in the corner with a little heater for warmth until they were big enough to go back out again. The black and yellow ducks might have as many as a dozen chicks, and I would often see them strutting round the yard with all their little ducklings strung out in a line behind. On one occasion a mother duck and her ducklings went missing, until some children came to tell us they were in the river quite a distance from the farm. They had swum down the farm's drain, gone nearly half a mile underground, and emerged totally unscathed in the river.

I can remember the animals at the farm but I don't recall any ever being slaughtered. If they were, the deed was probably done out of sight without my father telling me, which would have been tactful because children get attached to these creatures. I remember seeing a few hens that had been killed and were draining in the back yard, but it wasn't something that happened much – poultry wasn't as popular a food as it is today, and chickens were generally regarded as more productive if kept as layers.

This enterprise lasted only about five years before the land was needed for a new level (not private enterprise this time because the ground was compulsorily purchased), and what was left after they put in the roads and started digging the coal was not enough for a viable holding. So no more livestock farming for my father. It was back to basics, at which he was extremely good, producing on his allotment all the vegetables and fruit to adorn our table at home throughout the year.

There had been an allotment site adjacent to Llwynypia Hospital since 1917 and it had statutory status, which meant that it was protected in law. Anyone who wanted to cultivate a bit of ground – usually because they didn't have a garden of their own – had the right to apply for a plot and rent it for the purposes of growing food for themselves.

Although we paid our rent to the council, the land actually belonged to the farm that owned the whole of the mountain. To one side of the site was a tip where the National Coal Board dumped all the waste from the old Glamorgan Colliery, while at the top were the farm buildings and a golf course (also owned by the farm) that stretched for about six miles. As youngsters we would go up to the top of the mountain and search through the bracken for lost golf balls. Sometimes you'd find no end of them, and we would collect these in a bag and take them to the golf bar, where we'd get a few shillings for them.

Unlike today, when golf is a game for anyone, the sort of people who played golf then would be senior police officers, schoolteachers and professionals who had the time to spare. Ordinary people in the valleys generally worked six days a week with only Sunday off, so there was neither the leisure nor the energy to spare for golf.

For the same reason, the people you found on allotments tended to be manual workers who had retired, mostly men in their sixties who had the time to garden, and there were very few who were actually employed, as my father was. During the summer months especially, allotment gardening can be quite time-consuming. I'm not saying it's hard work (it isn't if you enjoy it), but if you were doing manual work all week it would be more difficult to set to on the plot on your one day off or in the evenings.

Another reason colliers tended not to be on the allotments was that most of them would grow their vegetables at home, in back gardens that were quite large by today's standards. We didn't fit into this typical pattern. Although our back garden was a reasonable size, my uncle kept show canaries and had two large sheds that occupied most of the ground there. The small remaining area was used for growing flowers.

So for us it was a choice between getting an allotment or going out to buy our vegetables. My father chose the former, hence our family's long association with allotment life. Even though my father was one of the youngest plotholders there in his early days, he loved the challenge of growing and I think he also enjoyed the peace and solitude you can find on your own little plot of land. And of course by putting food on the table for most of the year he helped supplement the family budget.

One distinct advantage of growing vegetables in your own garden at home was that housewives could do a bit of tidying up or weeding to help out, which they couldn't do on the allotments. In fact, I can hardly ever recall a woman coming through the allotment gate, let alone gardening on a plot, because it was strictly the men's domain. The only occasion you ever saw wives was when there was fruit to be picked. There was no rule explicitly barring women; it was just one of those features of the almost military style and discipline (chauvinism, it might be called today) of the committee men who ran the site.

Nor would you see any young people on the allotments. I was the sole exception when I took on my own plot at the age of eleven, and I don't remember, at least until the last decade, anyone under the age of forty or forty-five ever taking one. But that's all changing now.

When I first took on my own allotment at the age of eleven, both the older allotmenteers and all my mates thought it would be a flash in the pan. They knew I had a passion for growing vegetables but they thought my enthusiasm would soon fade. No chance! I loved the way of life *and* I could make money doing it as well. I still did all the same things as my mates, but my gardening enterprise meant I had more money than they did. The teasing and ribbing soon passed then, and those same friends in years to come were more than happy to ride in my car, bought as a result of my hard work on my plots.

When I was a child the allotment site was immaculate. There were forty-two plots altogether and a waiting list for vacancies. The plots were laid out on the hillside in three distinct tiers. A newcomer started in the far corner, at the top of the slope and the greatest distance from the gate, so he had to walk along several paths to reach the plot and transporting anything to it was hard work. It was a long way to cart it, and uphill as well.

This hierarchical arrangement was based on length of service. When anybody left the allotments for whatever reason, alive or dead, other plotholders could apply to move lower down, and that way you would start your descent down the hill and closer to the gate, at the same time creating a gap at the top for another applicant.

The site was managed by a committee, headed by Alf Daniel, owner of the blackcurrants I tried to scrump. He was a very tall man, without an ounce of fat on his body, sporting a long handlebar moustache and looking every inch the author-itarian he was.

Tommy Satchell was another who remains in my mind. He was our cobbler and he had a shed in his back garden where he repaired all the locals' shoes. His work left him with lots of leather offcuts and I remember seeing him digging his bean trench and burying all these offcuts in the bottom. To me it seemed a strange thing to do, because most of the members used only well-rotted manure in their trenches. (These days people put all sorts of things in the bottom of a bean trench to help conserve moisture.) But Tommy had a vast amount of this natural material available and this was a way of putting it to good use. He always grew good beans, so the method clearly worked.

Another imposing individual on the allotments was an Irishman by the name of Bob Cullen. It always seemed strange to me as a young boy that he had this soft accent that no one else shared, and a different way of speaking. Like the others, he was a very tall man. Perhaps there was something in the soil on the Rhondda hillside, which not only grew good vegetables but also sprouted tall men – it worked for me too, as I stand over six feet. Bob Cullen was very kind too. He grew lots of roses on his plot and as I was leaving the allotment he'd say, 'Do you want a bunch of roses for your mammy?'

These committee members were tall, lean regimentarians who reminded me of military men. They used to go round the whole allotment site on a Sunday morning, checking the plots and examining the paths. If your path was more than eighteen inches (45 cm) wide or not cleanly cut, or if there were any weeds growing on the plot, you were summoned before the committee and given a period of time in which to remedy this. If nothing was done after that, you were out: there was always a queue of people waiting for plots. In those days you could be kicked out in just a couple of weeks, whereas nowadays eviction could be delayed until the end of the year. In the majority of cases people knew they had to make improvements and a warning quickly brought them to heel. The committee would only take into account illness or perhaps some genuine problem within the family: the fact you just hadn't done the work wasn't acceptable. It was a system which might seem a little heavy-handed to us now, but it worked very well at the time and plots were generally kept in pristine condition.

Most allotment sites today are provided with a number of standpipes where plotholders can get water on tap for their crops, but ours has no mains supply at all. The mountain behind us is like a honeycomb, full of hollow chambers left from the coal levels, and that's where we get our water from: there's a constant flow draining the old workings and running out of the mountain, which amounts to a huge catchment area.

Just outside the top fence we've cut a big trench so that all this drainage water is channelled into a culvert. People sink plastic buckets or old containers in there, dip a hosepipe in their particular bucket and siphon out the water, which then cascades under gravity down the slope. The bucket in the trench is yours and it is your responsibility to keep it clear of silt, but because there are so many on the plots some of us share a bucket. For example, I share with Albie on the next plot above me, and I have my own pipe tapped into his supply and left in place down my path in the summer.

Albie's one of the truly long-serving plotholders, on the allotments since 1971. I knew him even before then because he lived in the house that backed immediately on to ours, and our back gates were in line. But I was only a passing acquaintance until I moved to my current plot immediately below his. After that he soon became a good friend and, as he retired before me, he regularly looked after my greenhouse and kept it watered while I was at work.

He's a man of few words and doesn't believe in using a sentence in reply if a simple 'yes' or 'no' will suffice. He's famous throughout our allotments for his habitual gym shoes and the range of bandanna headgear he wears to keep the sun off his thinning locks, and is fondly known among us as 'Johnny Dap' (Welsh slang for plimsolls is *daps*).

Like the rest of us, Albie started his gardening career on the upper plots, but now he resides on the second tier, one plot in from the gate. He has been there for many years and has no intention of leaving. He's got his buildings and plot exactly how he wants them and no longer has any desire to reach the 'promised land' just inside the gate: with his 'café' the meeting point for those on the lower plots, I think he is content to stay put.

To provide for the twenty-five gardening members these days there are about ten different water pipes, running everywhere like a maze of spaghetti, and the rest of us share. We usually pull them out of the stream for the winter, and then to start the water running again you have to suck hard at the end of the pipe, often getting a mouthful of silt and ending up coughing and spluttering. I remember once when Mickey, one of the lads there, was sucking and sucking at the end of his pipe.

'I can't get this water to come through,' he complained.

'Well, suck a bit harder,' we urged helpfully.

So he carried on sucking. Suddenly the obstacle came free, he staggered back and we could see this thing sticking out of his mouth. It was a dead mouse which had caused the blockage, and when it had finally come free it had shot into his mouth with its tail sticking out. He was coughing and heaving for ages after that, but at least he got his water running.

The only trouble with that water is that it is freezing cold, even on a hot summer's day, because it comes from deep inside the mountain. I feel that it chills everything if used direct – plants are like us and don't take kindly to being soaked in freezing water after standing in the warm sunshine all day. Instead I store it in a series of 45-gallon (200-litre) drums, which collect the rainwater from my glasshouse and overflow directly from one into the next. In summer I fill them with the mountain water one evening and wait until the next before using it, to give it time to warm up a little.

So that's our unique (and, so far, unfailing) water supply system. Another respect in which we differed from some other sites, in those days at least, is that we weren't allowed to keep poultry. At one stage the committee began to permit small poultry sheds on the lower plots as long as they were fully enclosed with runs, but some people started off on a small scale and then lost interest in gardening, so the amount of space the poultry took up started to expand.

Eventually these lower plots (which, being near the main gate, were the prized sites it might take you years to reach) became quarter- or even half-full of chickens. So the committee decided to get the poultry out altogether, and as anyone down there finished on their plot, whoever took over was not allowed to keep hens. At one point we got back to where we started, with all forty-two plots being cultivated solely for crops.

And then the Gas Board came through the top corner of the site with a new pipeline. This seriously disturbed the ground, which settled and sank afterwards, completely ruining it for the purposes of cultivation. About the same time the demand for allotments was dropping, and so that area was allowed to go gradually back to nature. That was in the sixties, when many of the original tenants were getting too old to do the work, and there was less interest among the up-and-coming generation (a problem affecting allotments nationally).

About a quarter of our plots went out of use or became derelict, and at one point we were lucky to keep the allotment site because the council was beginning to notice that so many were not being used. So to get the rent coming in again it was decided to allow poultry-keeping at the top. We didn't worry whether plots there were cultivated or not, just as long as they were kept tidy.

The advantage of this system is that the lower tiers of plots, where no poultry is allowed even now, are better protected. Plotholders at the top erected outer and inner fences to keep the poultry enclosed, and these are pretty high to stop the birds from escaping. So now we've got a complete barrier along the top, where the site is open to the mountainside, and this gives the lower two-thirds of the plots greater security.

Back in 1950, however, when I first started helping my father, all plots were fully cultivated and there were none of these problems. Dad's allotment was close to our house, and whenever he wasn't working he'd go up there, often for the whole day, because he grew a lot of fruit and vegetables and was very conscientious about looking after it all.

The half-hour allotment?

IT SEEMS TO ME that any idea you can manage an allotment in just half an hour or even half a day per week is wishful thinking. My father would be there for whole days at a time, and I find that from late April through to the middle of September I have to put in four or five visits a week – and that means an hour or so of work minimum at each visit. You don't want any interruptions either, so you might have to sneak in to make sure nobody stops you. *And* that assumes you've got a plot which is already tidy and in good condition.

Easy or low-maintenance gardening is a myth, and the 'half-hour allotment' isn't realistic if you're going to tend the plot well. For example, where do all these weeds come from? Even if your plot is reasonably clean ➜

they seem to travel miles just to settle on your soil and grow. I don't leave any weed to flower on my plot, to try and stop them perpetuating, but they still turn up. And if you are watering you need to spend a couple of hours in one session just doing that: it's no use just dampening the soil, you've got to give it a good soak because tickling just frustrates the plant.

I don't think you can keep an allotment well with just a little time each week, unless you revert to the old practice of zapping everything with chemicals and using lots of artificials, rotavating the ground and growing masses of potatoes and other big crops which will cover the surface, smother weeds and look after themselves.

I used to go with my father whenever possible and then make my own way back home when I'd had enough. As I got older I'd stay longer and longer, watching him and helping, and talking to neighbours on other plots (who tended to find me a bit of a novelty), taking an interest in what they were doing and growing.

In that way I started to discover the background to what I ate at home. For example, the major part of most plots was devoted to potatoes, which everybody grew in huge quantities because in those days people ate them every day. The typical meal each night consisted of hot food: a joint of meat – lamb, beef or pork, usually in rotation – together with cabbage, carrots or beans, and always unlimited potatoes. You didn't have pasta or rice or any of the other exotics, as we called them.

These meals were a fairly standard affair: the meat might change but there was little variation in the kind of vegetables, and any there might be depended on the time of year, because we always ate what was in season. My mother did her best to ring the changes, but one ingredient was constant: the liberal supply of potatoes.

Probably because the produce was cooked and consumed within hours of being picked, it always tasted delicious to me, and with all the energy I was expending I had a very healthy appetite, eating everything my mother put in front of me. I think it was a challenge to her to load my plate so full that I'd fail to eat it all, but I always rose to the occasion, so much so that she would regularly remark, 'I think you must have worms, the amount you pack away without putting on weight.'

She was an excellent cook and worked wonders with a limited budget. One of my favourite meals that she'd do in the summer was a huge plate of fresh runner beans, laced with plenty of butter, and a few large chunks of fresh bread. This is still a choice lunchtime snack for me to this day – just thinking about it makes my mouth water.

Broad beans were a popular crop that was always grown early. There were runner beans in summer (but no French beans until later years), cabbages (from spring and summer kinds right through to broccoli and savoys for the winter), and Brussels sprouts, swedes, parsnips and carrots were the main vegetables in winter.

With no freezers, we were unable to store much, and so everyone grew swedes and parsnips for the winter. Vegetables such as onions and potatoes were stored in a frost-free outhouse for winter use, while my mother preserved loads of shallots as pickling onions and made a whole range of jams from surplus fruit in summer. These all helped supplement the food on the table during the winter months, bringing back memories of sunny summer days on the allotment.

Despite what some people might assume about Welsh gardeners, I cannot recall in my early days on the plot ever seeing leeks being grown there. In fact they weren't too well known in the fifties, and my father didn't grow them until the 1970s. The leek may be the national emblem of Wales, but Rhondda gardeners certainly didn't grow them – what an unpatriotic lot! With no disrespect to my parents' generation, I suspect housewives didn't know what to do with leeks: certainly my mother never cooked them. To many they must have seemed strange long green things, somewhere between an onion and a cabbage. Vegetables generally went into a saucepan on the gas stove and were boiled, whereas to get the best out of a leek you need to cut it into 2-in (5-cm) chunks and put these round the joint to roast and develop their flavour in the oven. Even when making *cawl*, which always contains leeks now, many cooks tended to use onions instead.

Another reason leeks were missing was probably that no seed was readily available. You didn't get mail-order seed catalogues in those days and there were no supermarkets selling a big range of seeds, even as late as the seventies. Instead we used to go to the local ironmonger, who sold seeds loose: broad beans, runner beans and peas were all sold that way, and even cabbage seed was bought by the ounce (25 g). He had a small scoop and used to weigh up the seeds on his little scales, and you tended to grow whatever he had, which limited choice considerably.

There weren't that many different varieties available to us and you grew what everyone else grew. I remember 'Scarlet Emperor' was the only runner bean, for example, we all grew 'Ormskirk' savoys and the spring cabbage was 'Flower of

Spring', and you had very little option of growing anything else. The onions – 'Sturon' sets or seed – and 'Golden Gourmet' shallots were the same on every plot.

These days most allotments have a communal shed or shop where you can buy a whole range of seeds and equipment. We had a hut in the fifties, but this only really sold lime. Other things didn't come in until a decade or so later, when the Glamorgan Association of Allotments was formed, with their main store in Cardiff. All of us bought shares in the venture to help it start up, and they would trade in bulk to the allotments.

That was when bamboo canes and equipment like that began to appear on the scene. But even the association used to send up the seeds not in packets but loose in sacks for us to weigh out. Later they expanded their range of fertilizers to include sulphate of ammonia, bonemeal and Growmore, or National Growmore as it was called then. Like the lime, bonemeal and other fertilizers came in ordinary hessian sacks for weighing out, and this was as dusty as crazy. Nor were the sacks easily manageable because each weighed a full hundredweight (50 kg).

The hut was there strictly for business. There was no provision whatsoever for brewing coffee and sharing words of wisdom. Members were very kind and willing to pass on their information and experience, and they would always help each other. But they rarely sat down together to discuss the bigger issues of the world, and there was never the strong social element that is a popular part of the allotment scene everywhere today.

Most of the men, like my father, were simply too busy, because they were there for one purpose only, to grow the food they and their families depended on for their daily dinners. But I do believe that anyone who keeps an allotment for any length of time must also have an innate love of growing things. It never ceases to fascinate me that you can take a small amount of dust-like seed, bury it in the soil, see small green shoots appear as a result, and then watch them mature into wholesome vegetables to grace your dinner plate.

It is this bonding with nature and all things natural that makes gardening a lifelong passion, and you either love it or, as some strangely do, loathe it. That's why people come and go regularly on allotments, but there are always a few who make a lifetime of it.

Rules of the Partridge Road Allotments Society (c.1920).

1   The Society shall be called: 'The Partridge Road Allotment Society.'
2   That the Committee has the right to be the ruling body.
3   That each member's rent of 7/- [35p] per plot, per annum, be paid by the 31st March each year.
4   That all plots shall be fully cultivated except where allocated for keeping of poultry.
5   That each and every plot must have a path 18 inches [45 cm] wide, which must be kept clean, i.e. free from stones and rubbish. The paths to be kept clean are the bottom and left-hand paths looking towards the mountain.
6   That no trees shall overhang the paths.
7   That an allotment holder be allowed a tool shed and/ or a greenhouse, of reasonable size and appearance, but must apply for permission to erect same.

8   That we adhere to the National Allotment Law.

9   That the Annual General Meeting be held in November of each year, when all members are expected to attend.

10 These rules will be strictly enforced and any members failing to comply with same will be dealt with by the Committee, who have the right to give notice to quit.

Terry's Tip for February

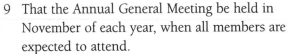

Waste not, want not

IF YOU ARE LIKE ME, all the old plastic labels you used for marking up the various plants throughout the season end up in a jumble in a tray on the greenhouse shelf or under the staging, covered with the written records of all the different varieties you grew during the year.

Don't throw them away! Take them indoors one wet day when you can't get on outside, and beg the use of the kitchen sink for an hour or two. Fill the sink with warm soapy water and let the labels soak while you make and drink a cup of coffee.

Then take a piece of fine wet-and-dry sandpaper and gently erase all the writing. Remember to clean off all the old soil too, because good hygiene is important when sowing seeds. Put the labels on the draining board until you have rubbed them all up like new, and then swill them thoroughly in clean water and allow to dry. →

With this annual treatment the same labels can be used over and over again for several years. What a tight lot we gardeners are!

Anthea's Recipe for February

Leek, Onion and Potato Soup

*T*HIS IS A GREAT *winter warmer, using vegetables that should be available fresh from the ground or out of store.*

* **2 large leeks**
* **2 medium potatoes, peeled and diced**
* **1 medium onion, diced**
* **1½ pints (900 ml) chicken stock or water**
* **½ pint (300 ml) milk**
* **2 oz (50 g) butter**
* **2 tbsp cream**
* **salt and pepper to taste**

Trim the tops and roots of the leeks and wash thoroughly, removing all soil; slice quite finely.

Gently melt the butter in a large saucepan, and add the leeks, potatoes and onion, stirring to mix them all together. Season with salt and pepper, cover and sweat over a low heat for 15 mins.

Add stock and milk, and simmer for 20 mins or until the vegetables are soft.

Pour the mixture into a liquidizer and blend to a purée; pour back into the saucepan and reheat slowly.

Serve with warm crispy bread. For extra colour, snip some chives on to the soup just before serving.

CHAPTER THREE

My Apprentice Years

FOR MANY PEOPLE in the fifties, growing your own food was one of the essential facts of life, not a hobby or leisure activity, and my father would go up to his plot as part of his responsibility of providing for us.

I already enjoyed gardening in all its aspects, so as often as not I'd be there with him, helping or amusing myself until I was bored. I never went there on my own or spent time unattended on his plot, because the gate was locked and he had the key. Anyway, I don't think the other members would have wanted to let me roam around too much on my own, at least to start with.

Right from the beginning I had my own little plot, a small piece of ground alongside my father's shed. About two yards square (3.3 sq m), it was an awkward patch sitting just where the path came round the shed. He never really wanted that bit for anything, so he used to put me on that and give me some tools to potter about with.

Then he would come along with a few odd plants or seeds and say, 'Here, put a couple of these or a couple of those in.'

They'd be mainly radish or lettuce, something that gives results fairly quickly and would keep my interest. So I'd put them in and keep an eye on them as they grew, and that was my real start in growing for myself. My main task was to help him, though, and he set me to work straight away, usually on a job he knew would instantly appeal to me as a child.

For example, he insisted on growing his Brussels sprouts in rock-hard ground. He reckoned if you could get a sprout plant in without a crowbar the soil wasn't firm enough, and with the old varieties that meant the sprouts would 'blow', turning into leafy rosettes like little loose cabbages instead of the solid balls of tightly packed leaves you expect with a well-formed sprout.

So to make the ground really solid before the plants went in he would get me playing cricket there with an old bit of wood and a tennis ball. Running back and forth on this patch of ground kept me entertained and gradually compacted the soil until it was rock hard. It's a method I can recommend!

It was the same with cauliflowers. The variety he used was 'All the Year Round', an old-fashioned kind now but one that's still available and worth growing. But it needs solid ground to make a solid head, otherwise the plants produce loose useless curds. Firm soil was something you had to have for older brassica varieties, whereas some of the modern hybrids have been selected and adjusted, I suspect, to be less fussy and grow in almost anything.

There were no expensive fertilizers available to us in those days. In fact, running an allotment needed very little outlay. The rent was seven shillings (35p) when I took on my first plot in 1957, and remained that way until the early eighties when the council compulsorily purchased the land from the farmer who owned it. (The rent then went up to £1, and increased by small amounts after that until now, in 2006, it is still only £14 for the year.)

We pay no water rates because our supply drains from the mountain and right through the plot. Seeds were relatively cheap when bought loose from the local ironmonger's. And supplying the fertility for the soil was all down to your own sweat and toil: you collected manure yourself or made your own compost, tasks that fell to me from a very early age.

The allotment outer fence was on the mountainside, and once over that you could go straight up into open country. There were no more fences after that; everyone had what would now be called walking rights up there, and for us kids it was a regular playground. Most of the time all you saw were free-range sheep, and one of my regular jobs was to go round with a bucket to collect all the sheep droppings, which my father would then put in a hessian sack and leave to soak in a barrel of water to make the liquid manure he used for feeding his runner beans.

And there was bracken up there, dense acres of it almost as far as you could see. During the school holidays my father liked to send me up on the mountainside to cut this bracken, which he then made into compost for putting back on the ground the following year. I had a scythe for cutting the bracken, a small half-moon sickle, and I had my own honing stone to keep the edge sharp. I'd bring it down eventually when it became really blunt, and my father would sharpen it properly for me, and then I'd go back up there and be cutting away the whole morning or afternoon on a good sunny day. Just think how many health and safety regulations I'd be breaking today.

My heap of cut stems would grow and grow as time passed, and then I would stick a huge pitchfork in, hoist up this great pile of greenery that almost hid me from sight, and come down the hillside to the allotment fence, where I tossed it over and went back for more. Once I'd brought it all down, I'd carry it along the paths to my father's plot, and add it to what had been gathered before.

I'd do that for the whole of the summer holidays, and by the end there would be a heap like a farm haystack. It would be huge, but as it decayed it gradually diminished and almost disappeared before your eyes: after only about five months that enormous stack would be reduced to a tiny pile on the ground, because bracken rots down to a very small amount. But it is very good for the soil, full of potash and rich in humus too. And it was there for the taking.

Holidays and spare time were not entirely filled with work, however, although gardening was something I never minded doing. I had a big group of friends. In the evenings I used to play with the kids in the street like everybody else, and during the school holidays I would go up the mountain with my jam sandwiches along with the others. It was a balanced life, and I had my playtime as well as the jobs on my father's plot. Even as a teenager, when I was building my allotment empire, I made sure there was always time to go out with my friends in the evenings.

All the time I was up there with my father I was learning, and being young I was quick to pick up everything he could teach me. He was one of those people who allow you to make mistakes without intervening. Although strict, he wasn't critical and never ran you down if you went wrong. The way he saw things, I'd got to learn, and that meant doing it myself, so he would often stand back and let me do something right or wrong, provided of course that nothing of his ever suffered. I can see he was right, because you learn more from your mistakes than from your successes: when things work out well, you just accept it, but when they don't you've got to analyse what went wrong, and you discover far more from working things out for yourself.

Of course, in gardening there may be no logical reason. Sometimes things just fail. You've drawn out a drill, chosen a reasonably new packet of seeds and sown them properly. You wait patiently and look week after week, but they never come up. You can't work out why, but something clearly went wrong although you don't know what it was. That's gardening, always a bit of a gamble even when you follow all the rules.

My father never gardened according to instructions on the seed packet, but preferred to watch the weather. Other people might read the packet and it would say to plant in April, perhaps, when the soil could be frozen or you might have a blanket of snow on the ground. He had this instinct – which I hope I've inherited – of knowing exactly when the soil conditions were ideal for sowing. He always believed that if you judged the conditions right, the seed would germinate well and grow into healthy specimens.

This was not an exact science. After a shower of rain, for example, when the ground looked nice and raked down to an even crumbly tilth, he'd say it was perfect. He'd sow his seeds then, and of course they would have just the right combination of warmth and moisture, so they would germinate promptly and grow quickly. And that was all he looked for. He never used cloches or anything like that to help things along. As a child I'd watch him and ask what he was actually looking for, and he wouldn't – or couldn't – tell me.

But I soon learned that if you could look at the soil and see it was nice, dark and moist, seed was going to grow. I've found since that, as well as going by appearance, if you simply rest the palm of your hand flat on the soil and it feels warm to the touch, then it is suitable for sowing; if it still feels cold, leave the seeds in the packet.

One valuable lesson Dad taught me was that gardening is all about patience: you have to wait for things to happen in their own time. Plants germinate, grow, flower and fruit when they are ready, not when you want them to, and you can't rush things.

As a youngster I found that hard at first. I used to put things in and then go and look at them every day, to see if anything was about to break through the surface. And then I'd start panicking if there was nothing there. But nothing happens until it's ready: plants have their own rhythms and a cycle from sowing to maturity, which is nature's domain, not ours.

My father taught me all the basics of gardening. He was a great advocate of winter digging, for example, and always liked to see his soil cleanly tilled during the winter months, except where his winter vegetables were growing or his fruit bushes were. This was part of his philosophy, which he instilled in me, that 'an hour spent during the winter months is worth five hours in the spring'. And he taught me the value of hoeing weeds on hot sunny afternoons, when they would quickly wither and die; this kept the ground weed-free with little effort.

He had what seemed to me to be a few odd little quirks, like insisting on planting his shallots on Boxing Day. He would always say that a shallot needed to be chilled, just like garlic, if it was to grow well. And in February he watched carefully for the right weather and soil conditions for sowing his parsnips. He reckoned that if you could get your parsnip seeds in then, when everything was just right, it didn't matter if there was a fall of snow afterwards because that would blanket the ground, trapping heat underneath to help them germinate, and as the snow melted they would be ready to benefit from the moisture and rising temperatures.

My mother rarely had to buy vegetables in those days, because my father aimed to grow everything we needed and usually succeeded. This meant growing fruit as well as vegetables, and he had a range of soft fruit on the plots – no trees but lots of raspberries, redcurrants, gooseberries and blackcurrants. He eventually added strawberries as well, although these were not so popular in those days.

The problem with strawberries was that they were best eaten on their own, whereas the other fruits could be made into more filling dishes. One of Mother's jobs was to turn the fruit into pies and tarts to have after your main course, because the daily cooked dinner would usually finish with home-made custard and a tart made with gooseberries, blackberries or whatever was in season.

I rate strawberries pretty highly, though. I consider there's nothing finer in summertime, when the vegetables and fruit are cropping well, than to sit at the top of my plot where I can admire the view up the valley, while I munch on a fresh-pulled carrot and a handful of young juicy peas, finishing off with a dessert of ripe sun-warmed strawberries straight from the plants. That makes everything worthwhile.

Fitting in strawberries

WHEN STRAWBERRIES ARE absolutely laden with white flowers during May they can look a real picture, full of the promise of long sunny days to come. I grow two full-length rows. Some of the plants are 'Honeoye', the leading commercial variety – early with a lovely-shaped fruit – and some are a home-grown allotment variety that lost its name but proved so good that it was passed round the plots. The plants don't crop well for ever: after three to four years vigour always declines and fruit size dwindles, so that the berries are then best used for jam. That's the cue to replace the plants, ideally around the longest day.

The trouble with planting strawberries is that the only ground spare in June for making a new bed tends to be where you've grown early potatoes, and you should never plant strawberries on ex-potato ground. So I tend to save a bit of ground specially for them, somewhere that I've used for a salad like lettuce and radish, perhaps. I let the strawberry runners root by themselves in the soil next to the rows of main plants, so that they form a more vigorous root system than they would do in pots. Then, in late August or September, when they are growing strongly, I can move good-size plants to freshly prepared ground, one variety a year to make sure of continuity.

Some things widely grown on allotments now were rarely seen then, if at all: tomatoes, for example, because nobody had a greenhouse. Almost every plot had a shed, and perhaps a cold frame, where people used to put their beans before planting them out. These were generally started in the shed and then moved to the cold frame as soon as they germinated. Nobody in my recollection ever sowed beans straight in the ground on the allotments, because slugs would be guaranteed to come and then you'd have lots of gaps. So everyone grew them indoors – in clay pots in those days, of course – and then transplanted them.

My father had a long narrow shed made out of old window frames, and in there he kept his chrysanthemums, both outdoor and indoor varieties, which he'd grow in big pots. These big incurved and reflexed varieties were moved outside for the summer and brought in again in September for cutting during November, December and January.

That was all I remember him growing under cover. As people acquired greenhouses, so tomatoes appeared, but that came later because there wasn't any means of providing heat, nor were there garden centres where you could buy tomato plants. So it was difficult to grow them until the advent of more up-to-date facilities. When we did, the only variety was 'Moneymaker', which was red and a good size, and that was enough for most people.

In those early greenhouse days we also used to try to grow cucumbers, but the only sort we had was 'Telegraph', and that needed checking regularly as the male flowers had to be taken off: if the females were pollinated the fruits were bitter. There were none of these modern hybrids that are all-female. Very often you would have a wonderful big cucumber but if you had missed just one male flower a single bee could do all the damage and the cucumber would be bitter.

As I got older I learned more and more, not just from my father but also from the other plotholders. I think they treated me as a bit of a novelty, because there was nobody else that young, and I was very interested and always asking lots of questions. All the old-timers were quite happy to pass things on – there was nothing secretive about them at all – and they taught me all they knew, in the same way, I expect, that their gardening knowledge had been handed down to them.

Apart from my father, the plotholder who possibly taught me the most about allotment gardening was Tommy Parr, a soft-spoken man who always had time to explain growing techniques to a newcomer. So of course I was always asking him questions, as youngsters do. And he would always start his answer with the expression 'there's no half and half about it'. Don't ask me where that came from or what it meant.

'Why have the lower leaves on my beans gone yellow, Tommy?' you might say.

'Well,' he'd say, 'there's no half and half about it, they've been chilled, but they'll soon pick up with a feed of super-phosphate.'

He was a showman who exhibited at many of the shows around the country, later becoming a judge, and he taught me a number of tricks for growing good vegetables. There was a great tradition of showing in the valley, but he was the only gardener from our allotments who exhibited vegetables; in fact there were probably only six or seven people in the valleys as a whole at that time who would regularly compete at all the local shows, sometimes even at venues throughout the UK. We had our own annual show, which goes on to this day in the Rhondda Sports Centre at the end of August. Anyone can enter if they've produced something that looks good, even though it might not have been deliberately grown for show.

Most of us grew to eat, or perhaps to sell, but for Tommy the main thing was getting that red card with 'First Prize' on it. That was his sole objective in growing, whereas we were more concerned to see how many beans we could get off that plant or, in my case later, how much money I could make. Tommy, however, was a showman to the core and the only member with the patience to master that strange art.

I remember distinctly the large onions he grew for the show bench. They were far superior in texture and size to anyone else's on the allotments. He always grew them in the same bed, which was prepared meticulously in the autumn with plenty of well-rotted manure. He was fortunate enough to have a greenhouse in his back yard at home, and always sowed his onion seed in there on Boxing Day – a way of escaping from the family for an hour during the festive season, I suspect.

He potted these on and on into larger pots until they were ready to be planted out in late April in this specially prepared bed, and then he would feed them with his own fertilizer mix for the next two months, to give the onions plenty of green top shoots. This mixture was a closely guarded secret, although he told me once it was based on sulphate of ammonia and potash. He never divulged the proportions of the mix.

So great was the renown of his onions that among the stuff stolen when the allotments were broken into once were two large bunches of Tommy's onions. Several days later the police raided the house of a known felon, and in his kitchen were hanging two strings of superb onions. The police knew immediately they weren't his, recognized them as Tommy's and returned them to their rightful owner. Such are the rewards of fame.

To show well, you need to grow well. I learned the essentials of good ground preparation for each vegetable type from Tommy, and he gave me some of the basic tips needed to get good germination of seed. He would spend an infinite amount of time preparing the site for each of his show-bench crops, studying its preferences to find out the nutrients it needed and then making sure the right balance of feeds was added to the soil.

He tended to prepare his soil with much more inorganic fertilizer than anybody else. He'd use lots of potash and sulphate of ammonia, for example, because he wanted high-quality appearance rather than flavour. It was essential that his vegetables grew quickly and looked good, and taste was secondary.

The rest of us would add manure if we had it, and if we hadn't, well, we simply wouldn't. Perhaps we'd give cabbages a handful of sulphate of ammonia to make them grow quicker, or add some superphosphate to the runner beans to make their flowers set, but this was always on an ad hoc basis. Tommy, on the other hand, studied the form, knew what he was looking for and gardened accordingly.

Something that always intrigued me was the huge amount of vegetables he used to get ready to find the right combination for the show bench. He would pick dozens of runner beans to find six of good length and size, which he used to wrap in damp tea towels to keep them supple and straight. Similarly with potatoes, he would dig a hundred to get six perfect specimens. So he grew large amounts of everything to find the right quantity for the show bench. And again, he built lots of shelters on his plot, constructing a wooden frame over his onions, for example, to keep the weather from marking the skins.

Winning is not just about appearances, though: how you

present your entries can count for just as much, and Tommy would be up there for hours sometimes, grooming his entries. He used to show sweet peas and chrysanthemums – I've still got some of the green flower vases he staged them in, which he gave me when he left – and he'd go up there and after a lot of searching he'd finally pick six chrysanthemum blooms. Then he'd spend ages with a tiny paintbrush patiently opening every single petal until each flower looked perfect.

I never really got interested in all that, but I learned a lot from watching him. He willingly passed on information because he knew there was nobody else on the plots to compete with him, and he certainly appreciated that I wasn't a serious rival: he might have been a bit more guarded if I had been.

Something he would never share with you, though, was the surplus of his show stuff. If he had a load of beans and had chosen his six for the show bench, he wouldn't give you any of the others – these he would take home to cook or simply throw away. You couldn't get hold of anything he didn't want. Anything that was not intended for show he would give you, just like anybody else with a surplus. But if he had a row of beans for show, he'd go up there on Friday night to pick and check and measure them, and then take home all those he had rejected. It was the same with potatoes: after he had selected his six perfectly clean, uniform specimens, the dozens of others he had dug he'd take home.

He'd never give you any of the onions he didn't want either, and there were plenty of those. He was a master of the art of preparing them for show, peeling off the outer layers until the bulbs looked evenly brown and shiny. The roots were left on, but carefully teased out to look clean and white and a uniform length. Then he would chop off the tops at a particular point so that they were all trim and immaculately matched.

Those big onions might have looked impressive but they were not good keepers, and by the end of the summer would go rotten if you hadn't eaten them. They were a special variety grown from seed and fed for size, whereas the rest of us grew ours from sets, mainly to produce an average kind of bulb that we could string and confidently store through the winter.

I would not insist that large size always sacrifices flavour because sometimes you can have both, but on the whole growing with the intention of producing unnatural dimensions means giving away the taste. To achieve your aim you have to do some things almost to excess, which is not what gardening's really all about.

I'm a great believer in letting a plant extract what it can from the soil, nurtured by water and by the sun, growing slowly and in that way building in the flavour. If it is grown fast and furiously, I think it will lack something. Throw a handful of sulphate of ammonia on a cabbage, for example, and it will grow large and dark green and look luscious, but it will not have taken in the flavour of the sun in its own time.

But that is a viewpoint which combines my father's insistence on patience and my later conversion to organic fertilizers. At that time I was still learning everything, and I soaked up all the information I could get. One of Tommy's tips that has remained with me is the way he used to tie bean canes together, using a single piece of string so that the strength of the tie holds them all taut, however strong the wind. This is a method I still follow to this day, a well-honed procedure that some plotholders regularly come and ask me to do for them.

In time most of the plotholders who had been gardening there for many years became fatherly figures, and freely passed on all their accumulated knowledge to me. In my turn I have willingly passed that on to any newcomers who are prepared to listen. But I started off by absorbing my father's gardening experience and wisdom, and I shall be ever grateful to him for that, because much of my knowledge and understanding of gardening I owe to him.

I kept that original little square by the shed where I had first started when I was four, even after my father had let me help out with other things. Eventually he would ask me to go and till a piece of ground here, or rake somewhere else ready for sowing, or go and put in a row or two of seeds. He would always watch what I was doing, and he'd never let me run riot. On his plot I was supervised in whatever I was doing, and if I did it wrong he would tell me in good time, because that was his ground and the vegetables he grew there were important.

Once I was eleven and took my own plot, though, I had to learn my lessons myself and he didn't intervene at all. His attitude was different then: you'd ask if you wanted to know, and if you didn't ask he'd assume you knew. If it didn't work, you learned. But it wouldn't be his loss then, it would be mine.

Terry's Tip for March

Sowing hints
AS YOU START SOWING seeds this month, remember my father's advice and don't treat the instructions and sowing dates on the back of seed packets as gospel. The important information to note with any vegetable is the time a particular variety takes to grow from sowing to harvest. Even this is only an average for normal conditions, but it does give you a rough idea to help you plan your schedule. →

If you want crops early, then sow at the earliest possible date, but make sure the soil is warm and moist, and cover the seeds with cloches or fleece in a cold season. Later sowings often catch up, if you miss or lose earlier ones. For the longest cropping season sow little and often, and protect the first and last sowings to extend the season a little. Most seeds germinate and grow fastest in the long summer days, but start to slow down as the days shorten from August onwards.

When faced with the full extent of an allotment, most beginners sow long rows of seeds right across the plot, which soon fills the ground, results in a lot of weeding and aftercare, and may yield more than you can use while it's in peak condition. If you can give lots away or preserve it, this might be a good arrangement, but for a steady yield sow shorter rows (or part-rows) more often: they're easier to manage, and you can often fit more in by resowing or planting as each short row is cleared.

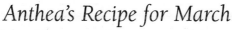

Anthea's Recipe for March

Rhubarb Jelly Special

IF YOU FORCE IT under boxes and buckets for early sticks, there should be enough fresh rhubarb to pull this month for its subtly delicious flavour. Alternatively you might have frozen or bottled rhubarb left from last season, and perhaps even a few cooking apples still in store. This dessert turns them into something a bit special, with a hint of all the fresh fruit you could be gathering in the not too dim and distant future.

* **1 lb (450 g) rhubarb**
* **1 lb (450 g) cooking apples**
* **1 packet of jelly (raspberry or strawberry)**
* **½ cup of water**
* **brown sugar to taste (approx. 1 tbsp)**

Wash and trim the rhubarb, and chop into small pieces. Peel, core and slice the apples.

Put the rhubarb and apple in a saucepan with the water and sugar, and cook until tender and pulpy.

Cut or tear the jelly into squares, add to the saucepan and stir until completely dissolved.

When the jelly and fruit are completely mixed, pour into individual dishes and leave until set. Serve with fresh cream or ice cream.

CHAPTER FOUR

Empire Building

R IGHT FROM THE START, taking on my own allotment was intended to be a money-making venture. This seemed to me an ideal arrangement: I could continue with my enjoyable hobby and convert some of the pleasure into good pocket money. It was like having your cake and eating it, the best way with everything!

As youngsters we rarely got any pocket money. When we went to school, we'd have our dinner money and sometimes a small amount to spend, but never very much and it certainly wasn't guaranteed: we couldn't be sure we were going to get it every week. If you did have money it was usually because you'd earned it in some way at home. There was always something you had to do for that couple of pence, because you weren't given money for nothing.

Delivering the daily newspapers was a traditional and simple way for youngsters to earn some pocket money, and I was eleven years old when I started my paper round. A friend of mine, John Rees, who was later best man at my wedding, already had one, and said to me one day, 'There's a job going in the paper shop, if you want a paper round.' It was something I had always wanted to do, so I was there like a shot.

I started on a weekly wage of 2/6d (12½p), working early every morning from Monday to Saturday. There was an extra delivery on Friday evenings for those people who had magazines but bought no dailies, and that was also when I collected the money. I used to call in at the shop on my way home from school on a Friday night and pick up a leather satchel and a book listing all my customers, marked up with the weeks. People were expected to pay their bills every Friday, or if anyone missed a week they had to pay double the following week. By the time I finished that Friday evening round, there must have been quite a bit of money in my bag, but you never thought in those days about getting mugged for all that change you were carrying about.

Bob Hands, who ran the post office and paper shop, had an old dark-green Rover, one of those round-topped models built like a tank. Each morning he'd get you to put your papers in a sack, then he'd load these in the back of his car and take you to the start of your round, which might be quite a distance along the valley. Boys who were more local walked, but as I started about a mile away he would drop me off and I'd then walk back to where I lived.

What truly amazes me when I look back is that, compared with now when every daily paper contains full television listings, in those days everybody bought a copy of the *Radio Times*; when ITV came along, they'd buy the *TV Weekly* as well.

Comics such as the *Eagle*, the *Beano* and the *Dandy* were popular too. Then there was the local *Rhondda Leader* on a Friday, and you could reckon that 90 per cent of those who took a daily paper would have a *Leader* as well. And there were all the women's magazines, such as *Woman's Own*. Almost everybody bought some kind of magazine, so the paper bag used to be quite heavy most mornings, and again on Friday evenings.

John and I would also get together to make money picking blackberries up the mountain. In those days tomatoes came in hardened cardboard baskets with a metal handle at the top, and these were ideal for picking fruit. Up just beyond the top of Llwynypia Hospital there were a lot of wild brambles, and we would go up there, fill our baskets with berries and then go round the streets selling them at the door. I think we charged about a shilling (5p) for a half-pint (300-ml) glassful, and we'd do that all through the blackberry season.

At Christmas John and I formed a two-man choir and went out singing carols around the local streets. On New Year's Eve we'd be out at midnight knocking on doors and wishing the partying occupants a happy new year, to earn an extra bob or two.

So John and I were already earning regularly when we were eleven, experienced entrepreneurs at that early age and always interested in new money-making ventures. Perhaps it was inevitable, then, that John would realize taking on a plot at the allotments might be another good way to make some extra income during the summer months.

'Why don't we share one?' he suggested one day.

The trouble was that only one tenant could have a plot and officially you weren't allowed to share. There's nothing in the rules to say somebody else can't help you, but the plotholder has to be solely responsible, to avoid any arguments about who owns which bit and who should be doing what.

We decided I would take a plot as I was already known up there, and I told my father what I wanted to do. He looked sceptical at first, and it must have seemed a bit early to him. But I'd been pottering around on his plot from the age of four, so I had a bit of knowledge by then and was familiar with most things that were grown on the site.

Finally, when a plot became available at the top, he said, 'OK. You'd better send a letter in to the committee then, to apply.'

There was no interview, and the committee met behind closed doors. They didn't invite you to meet them – if you didn't get a plot, that was that, there was never any explanation. Even now there's never an interview for a plot. People put in for one, the letters are dated in order of application, and we do a bit of enquiring into what the person is like and who knows him, and whether he (or these days she) is trustworthy. The committee would never take anyone unknown, but in the valleys somebody on the allotments would be sure to know you. And the committee all knew me, of course, because I was in there all the time, so there was no problem.

The others on the allotments couldn't believe it, though, and there was a bit of humming and hawing about letting an eleven-year-old have a plot on his own. But my father was on the committee at the time, and he said I was always up there and always asking questions, so why not give me a chance?

They probably realized they had nothing to lose, and if I didn't last long it wouldn't be a disaster. When you took over a plot it was always relatively clean. People never clung on to them until they were so derelict that anyone new coming in had to start at square one. The regime was so rigid that if the plot did deteriorate, they would put pressure on the member to sort it out or leave. If there was no sign of anything happening after that, they would quickly evict, so you always took on a plot in reasonably good condition. They would soon let me know if things went wrong.

My father obviously swung it and they allocated me a plot up near the top, a good place to be because you had first access to the water up close to the top fence. But anything else I needed, such as manure, was hard work to bring in because I was almost the farthest I could possibly be from the gate and had to climb up the hill to reach the plot.

So we started our new money-making venture, and John came along to help me, full of enthusiasm at first. But he had never been interested in gardening, nor had his family, and he had underestimated the amount of work it needed and couldn't get into it. He hadn't realized you had to dig for a start, or that you had to spend to get something back. The main attraction for John had been that growing to sell seemed a good way to increase his earnings in the summer months, to supplement the couple of shillings he was already making from his paper round. In a short space of time he just disappeared: we started in the spring of 1957, and by the time we were getting busy, about June, he'd completely lost interest. I was left with the whole plot, all to myself.

It seemed a lot of ground, but the advantage was that it was clean and I was enthusiastic. And it didn't take long after school to walk the hundred yards up there from home and put in some work. My paper round gave me the money to buy anything I needed, and it was always possible to scrounge off my father the odd half-packet of cabbage or carrot seeds, or any potatoes he had left over – he'd buy a whole sack of seed potatoes and there would usually be some to spare.

It was the same with runner bean plants, because everybody puts in that extra few as a fallback, in case there are a few gaps later. If you had a full germination you would have half a dozen or so plants that were not wanted, and I used to get all the leftovers. This sharing and passing on was all part of the traditional allotment culture. The advantage was that we all grew the same varieties: I dread to think what might happen these days if you were to scrounge three plants here and four there, because you could end up with a row of runner beans containing as many as fifteen varieties, all performing differently.

It was hard work, especially in the summer when the vegetables started cropping ready for sale. It was that which really put John off. We were both up early every morning of the week doing the paper round, but there were no Sunday papers to deliver. John didn't want to get up and go to the allotment on a Sunday morning: with no school and no paper round, that was his day off and he could have a couple of extra hours in bed. But I was selling, so on Friday nights I was there in the summer harvesting the crops and preparing what I was going to take out the next morning. On Saturday mornings I would be delivering, and Sunday mornings I was doing all the routine cultivation work. There was a pattern, even if a demanding one.

As often happened, I proved that my father was right. Part of the secret of staying on top of the work was to keep up to date with winter preparation, because whatever I could do in advance saved a lot more time and effort later on in the busiest season.

My allotment customers were all local. Word soon spread that I had stuff to sell, and I used to go round asking neighbours if they wanted any beans or potatoes, or whatever was ready. At my peak, when I had ten plots, I had between fifteen and twenty-five regular customers throughout the summer, but there were others who used to come up to the allotments and ask if there were any beans to spare. They'd be people in the street who didn't have plots, and who simply came to the gate and asked, 'Anybody got anything to sell?'

Everyone up there on the allotments sold something, but none of them on a guaranteed weekly basis like I was doing. They'd just sell their surplus, whereas I had no surplus as such because everything I grew was for sale anyway. My father was providing all we needed for the house. Occasionally he would have more than we needed, and if I was short I'd add it to my orders. But mine was the only plot that was quite openly a business.

The rules of the allotments stated that all produce was strictly for the plotholder's own use – that still applies today – but nobody really objected because growing for sale was keeping the ground under cultivation. I think at first some of the older members were a bit dismayed that I was effectively breaking the code about selling produce, but everyone was doing it to some degree, so it would have been hypocritical to complain and might have compromised their own activities.

I was soon earning good money. It was only about three months before I was able to start digging potatoes and cutting cabbages, and by late June I was already into the peak of the runner beans, always a popular vegetable with customers. I grew only what I could sell, and in those days people's requirements were fairly narrow; there wasn't the huge range of different crops and varieties. The demand was for potatoes, runner beans, cabbages and carrots. Nothing much else was readily available as seed. People's eating habits did not include 'fancy' vegetables and as there were no supermarkets no one had heard of peppers, courgettes and aubergines. Herbs were limited too, and most people used only mint and sage. Even parsley was a bit exotic then.

I didn't have a bicycle or any other means of transport, and simply carried the orders to people's houses. I used the trays that tomatoes came in from Guernsey, flat wooden ones with four triangular corners, and I could stack two or three of these on top of each other to take out at a time. Sometimes, especially if people had ordered a lot of potatoes, they could be too heavy and then I'd have to take them one at a time. But I never had to carry them that far because the streets were all pretty close together, and all my regular customers lived nearby.

That first plot I kept for a couple of years before another became available. Nobody wanted that, so I took it on as well, which increased the amount I could raise and sell. Then another fell vacant. I took that, too, and my empire began to grow, especially in my mid-teens when allotment membership was diving.

Circumstances and attitudes were beginning to change at the turn of the 1960s. New industry with its higher wages was moving into the valleys to replace the declining coal mines, women were going out to work and so many families now had more money coming into the house. With this increased disposable income people wanted to go out and enjoy themselves. Gardening seemed hard work in comparison and was time-consuming. At the same time the older long-term tenants were beginning to find that keeping a plot under control was increasingly difficult and they were dropping out, just when the allotments didn't seem to be attracting anybody new.

So the 'swinging sixties' were good for my business. Whenever a plot became vacant I would take it on, until by the time I was sixteen or seventeen I had ten under cultivation (and Tommy Parr had eight).

As I took on more allotments, I'd increase my quantities, which made planning much easier: instead of dividing an area up into different crops, I could put a whole plot down to potatoes or beans or cabbages, all of which still formed the bulk of my orders. Rather than expand into other crops for which there was little or no demand, I stuck to the things which were easy to sell and to grow. If I could put a whole plot down to potatoes, for example, there was little to do other than dig the ground, plant the tubers and then go through with a hoe occasionally. Otherwise they almost grew themselves and tended to keep the plot clear of weeds.

A whole plot of cabbages was simple to manage too. I needed to keep a good succession of maturing heads going because I was cutting over a long period to meet demand. I'd use the same varieties ('Primo' or 'Winnigstadt') all the time because growing other kinds would have meant messing around with different cutting times. All I had to do was start a fresh batch every three or four weeks. I would sow these in a drill to one side, thin them out and then sow more as the young plants reached the transplanting stage.

Even with a lot more ground at my disposal, it was still very difficult to get the right balance and a steady supply of vegetables. I couldn't always predict the season or the demand, and some weeks I'd be struggling to fulfil orders, especially for potatoes, which everybody bought in large quantities. Some years I'd run out altogether halfway through the season, while the beans or cabbages were still cropping well.

My solution was to go to the local wholesaler on a Friday night and pick up however many bags of potatoes I needed to complete the orders next day. Then I'd dig a big hole in the plot, tip all the potatoes in, heap the earth back on top and spray the lot, absolutely soaking them with water, and then leave them all night. When I dug them up the next morning, they'd have earth on them and look as though they were mine. And the customers would always say they could tell the difference with such fresh produce!

A matter of good taste

THE STANDARD COMMENT from my customers the next time I went round to deliver would be, 'Oh, I'm glad I had this from the allotments. The stuff's always better than what you can buy in the shops.' Even now people often say that vegetables tasted better long ago or that they have more flavour when grown organically or by someone you know.

How much of that was psychological, the result of knowing where the stuff was grown, I don't know. There was no organized organic movement on the allotments in the early sixties to offer any comparison, and people were making those comments even while I was using artificial fertilizers and insecticides.

I do wonder if the reason wasn't really much simpler, and that good flavour has a lot more to do with produce being on the plate within hours of harvest rather than lingering in the shops, maybe for days. This was certainly why my father went up on Christmas morning to gather the veg for dinner, and why I started off married life doing the same.

Although there were sometimes small hiccups in supply, especially with potatoes, I can't remember any occasions when I seriously failed to meet demand in the peak season. There were always years when the season began late or finished sooner than usual, and then I would break the news to some of the customers that, for example, I was starting to run out of beans now and probably wouldn't have any more for that week. But the better customers, the ones who were regular and always looked after me, I tended to keep supplying as long as I could.

My busiest time I reckoned to be from June, when the first early potatoes came ready, until September, with a peak for about nine weeks during the bean season, from early July onwards.

Even though everyone used them, I didn't grow onions because they took up the ground from late March through to mid- to late August before they were ready, and by then everything else would have been starting to run down. I suppose I could always have bought a bike and a beret, strung them from the handlebars and hawked them round the houses, but basically they did not fit well from a commercial angle.

Similarly I didn't sell in the winter. It's difficult to predict demand for winter vegetables, and with so much to grow to meet the summer trade there was never the space to grow winter crops. Whereas I tended to concentrate on harvesting from June through to September, a crop like parsnips would go in during March and I wouldn't be digging them until the autumn. In the winter there wouldn't be the daylight on a Friday evening to go up and harvest them.

I could not have supplied enough maincrop potatoes anyway, and once I stopped offering them customers would go somewhere else. Some people would have 20 lb (9 kg) per week because of the vast amounts they used at every meal, and even then they might come back for more in the middle of the week. When you've got a family of four, five or six you can get through a lot of potatoes if you cook the same basic meal every night. Other vegetables, too: I'd often pick 2 cwt (100 kg) of beans regularly on a Friday night.

Sometimes I might plant some very late cabbages as a

successional crop to follow an earlier batch, or perhaps put some spring cabbage in to start the next season along with a few of the earliest potatoes that might be ready for harvesting in May. But on the whole the plots tended to be empty during the winter, and that was when I did my digging, turning all the ground over.

One huge advantage of having several plots was that it made life simple from the point of view of rotating crops, moving everything round regularly to avoid a build-up of pests and diseases. Some gardeners undervalue rotation, but it's something I've always done, initially within my first plot and then, when I had more, by rotating whole plots at a time. This was a particularly important way to keep crops healthy in the late fifties and early sixties because we didn't have many remedies for controlling diseases, and rotation was recognized as the best precaution. Having my empire made this much easier because I would mark off complete plots for a single crop; otherwise I had to rely on memory or keep a record on paper to remember what I did the previous year.

I made a profit from the original allotment in my first year, and by the time I was market gardening in earnest I was probably earning a good £300–400 per season – and this was at a time when I was selling runner beans for about 6d (2½p) per pound. In fact I remember thinking when I started my first job that I was earning £6.4s.8d (£6.23) a week at work before stoppages (paid in cash in a little brown envelope!), whereas I earned more than that selling my allotment produce, something I enjoyed much more too. But of course that didn't apply throughout the year.

I always kept the money in the house because in those days you didn't trust banks. Everything was done with cash, anyway, not cheques or bank cards, so if you had anything to save you simply kept it in a tin. And it would usually stay there: there was nothing much for a youngster to spend it on, apart from the odd few sweets for yourself. Over the years while I was at school the money accumulated, so that by the time I was seventeen I had enough to buy my first car.

236 RTX

As soon as I was seventeen I started having driving lessons (something else my allotment money paid for), and my brother, who already owned a Ford Anglia, used to teach me whenever he came home from his teaching job in Wimbledon.

I passed my test second time, and the minute I had that driving licence I bought the car, a three-gear Ford Popular (100e engine, registration number 236 RTX) that cost me all of £236, paid for in cash from my allotment and paper round savings. It was bright canary yellow all over, which went well with my fashionable fluorescent socks, and was known by everyone as 'Walt's Wagon'.

Gaining my own wheels at the age of seventeen gave me a great sense of achievement and seemed a handsome payback for all my endeavours. There were not many cars on the valley roads in the early sixties, so I was among the elite. It certainly impressed my schoolmates, who all joined me regularly on our little excursions outside the valley, although I have to say it didn't seem to impress the valley girls much. Perhaps the bright colour clashed with their lipstick.

My father had plenty to do on his own allotment growing the food for the household, but he took a great interest in what I was doing and managed to get more involved as I took on extra plots. He'd often say, 'Well, what else can we grow now?'

It was thanks to him and his enthusiasm that I branched out and got involved in growing flowers, because he reckoned there was more money to be made there. This was a novel idea to me. I regarded my allotments as a solely vegetable enterprise, whereas he had always grown flowers as well – sweet peas, dahlias and chrysanthemums of all kinds in pots for flowering indoors. And it was he who spotted their money-making potential.

The first kind we tried were sweet Williams, a semi-early flower ready for cutting in May and June, and lasting for ages in water. My father already knew a lot about them and had grown several long rows the year before. As they are biennials, sown in May for planting out in summer to bloom the following year, I could fit them in as I cleared the rows of early potatoes. I put masses in that first year.

They're an extremely colourful and highly scented flower with instant impact. They have a large, sturdy head of multi-coloured blooms, some, like the fabulous auricula-eyed kinds, with concentric circles of contrasting colours. Not surprisingly, there was a tremendous and immediate demand for them. I sold them around the streets, and on a Sunday afternoon I used to go and stand outside Llwynypia Hospital selling them from buckets.

That was so easy. The hospital is about 300 yards from the allotment gate, so all I had to do was cut and bunch the flowers, take six or seven buckets down there with me, and then wait for the people coming to visit. In those days hospital visiting was restricted to Sunday afternoons between two and three o'clock. During the rest of the week matrons used to stop anyone other than close relatives from going to a bedside, and then only one, occasionally two people were admitted at a time.

On a Sunday, however, whole families could go, together with children or grandchildren. So there were always plenty of people wanting to take a gift into the wards, and as this was before chocolates or grapes became so popular they would buy a bunch of flowers. With visiting limited to just one hour, people tended to arrive on time or early, so as long as I was there and set up by one thirty I could reckon to be sold out and gone by a quarter past two.

That was the start, and a very successful one. Those long rows of plants neatly followed the potato crop, transplanted straight into the fertile, well-broken-up soil, and then cropped heavily the following spring over two or three weeks at their peak. I'd keep them for a second year and then scrap them after cutting all the blooms. Each year I sowed more to keep a steady annual supply, collecting some of the seed myself – sweet William seed is extremely plentiful – and also buying in some fresh annually.

Next we saw the potential for summer flowers, and started growing dahlias in large quantities. They are another wonderful cut flower and did very well. Then we got in touch with a florist in Tonypandy who had a steady demand for sweet peas and roses, and eventually two plots were put down just to roses. My father knew of a big rose grower in Norfolk, close to where his sister lived on the farm, and we bought our rose bushes from there wholesale.

The florist used to come in and pick what I always thought were rubbish, the short-stemmed blooms that were in fact ideal for working into bouquets or wreaths. She wanted tight buds and only certain colours, the reds, pinks and whites, and would come up to cut them herself and then tell me how many she'd taken if I wasn't there. She had her own key and used to come on a Friday or Saturday morning, or any other time in the week if she had a special order, and then go and snip all she wanted, whether it was two dozen or fifty or more buds.

I grew sweet peas, too, going up the mountainside and cutting twiggy branches from the willows to support the climbing plants. Some of these summer flowers I sold to people who came into the allotments looking to buy a bouquet or make one up for a birthday or some other special occasion. I became quite adept at making bouquets myself, and I'd use the maidenhair fern that grew around the waterholes on the allotments and the gypsophila ('gyp' to florists) which we grew in cut-off empty oil drums to make the finished bouquet look big and impressive.

But the surplus I gave to my customers, adding them to the top of the pile of vegetables I was delivering, as a sweetener. Most people were still thrifty in the early sixties and didn't like paying good money for a bunch of flowers to put in the best front room, however much they wanted them. So I'd just slip these flowers in with the order.

'We didn't ask for any flowers,' they would say.

'No,' I'd agree, 'but you're a very good customer and as a token of my appreciation I've cut these just for you.'

And then I'd get a healthy tip, often more than the value of the flowers themselves.

Terry's Tip for April

Starting runner beans

THIS IS THE MONTH when allotment gardeners make their first runner bean sowings, in pots indoors for an early start and to avoid the common problems with sowing direct into the soil. Most of us have difficulty at some time or other with germination, especially in a cold season, or from marauding slugs, particularly on wet ground. The result is gaps in the rows, always an irritation as well as a waste of space.

But even sowing in pots isn't 100 per cent successful, and you can find several are left empty by seeds that do not germinate.

The best way to ensure a full batch and no waste is to fill a strong, clear plastic bag with moist, fresh seed compost. Open the seed packet and tip all the beans into the compost, stir well and then tie the top of the bag to keep the moisture in. Put the bag somewhere warm and keep a careful eye on the contents.

As soon as you see the small white taproots emerging from the beans, tip them out and plant each bean gently in an individual small pot – about 3 in (8 cm) diameter is ideal. Any that have not yet germinated can be reburied in the bag of compost and left in the warmth for a little longer. You can use this method with any other large seeds, like peas and French beans.

When you come to transplant the beans outdoors, position one plant at the base of each cane, and another between every pair of canes. These inter-mediate plants can be left to make their way to one side or the other, to climb whichever cane they choose. →

(The canes should be about 9 in (23 cm) apart.) The extra plants thicken up the rows and boost the overall crop, but you do need rich fertile soil to sustain all this extra growth.

Anthea's Recipe for April

Rhubarb and Ginger Jam
(900w microwave recipe)

NEXT MONTH IS THE start of the real fruit season, with green gooseberries ready to thin for cooking and the first strawberries coming on stream. Until then there's only rhubarb available, but what a valuable crop, one you can force really early indoors, cover outside to follow on and then leave to grow in the open for the rest of the season. Before you're seduced by the strawberries, pull some extra rhubarb for making this simple but succulent microwave jam.

* 2 lb (900 g) fresh rhubarb
* 2 tbsp of water
* grated zest and juice of 1 orange
* grated zest of 1 lemon
* 2 lb (900 g) sugar
* 1 oz (25 g) fresh root ginger

Wash and trim the rhubarb, and cut into 1 in (2.5 cm) lengths. Place in a 5-pint (2.8-litre) bowl with the water, citrus zest and juice. Cover and microwave on high for 10–12 mins or until soft, stirring at least once.

Microwave the sugar on low to warm for 6 mins, and then stir into the rhubarb until dissolved.

Beat the ginger with a rolling pin to break down the fibres and release the flavour. Tie in a muslin bag and add to the rhubarb.

Microwave uncovered at high for 35–38 mins or until the setting point is reached, stirring three times. Remove the muslin bag.

Cool for 5 mins, then ladle into sterilized jars, seal and label.

CHAPTER FIVE

The Pencil Factory

LIFE DURING MY TEENS was full to overflowing. I was tall and thin, six foot two with more bones than a kipper, and there wasn't an ounce of fat on me because I never stopped burning energy, from the early hours of the morning until sometimes eleven o'clock at night.

I was at the grammar school then, so I had to plan everything around my homework. There was no chance to waste time, never an opportunity just to sit and do nothing, unlike these days when we might relax in front of the television. We didn't have that, and the day was filled instead with physical activities or homework or going out enjoying myself. Somehow it all fitted quite compactly into my life.

We were fitter in those days, I'm certain. No one ever seemed to get a cold, perhaps because the house was not centrally heated and so we were never exposed to a vast range of temperatures. And we ate plenty of good food. Dieticians go on now about the need to eat five daily portions of fruit and vegetables – well, we might not have had the range of fruit but we certainly had many portions of vegetables each day as a matter of course.

We all tended to eat fatty food as well. The meat was generally red and not lean at all, and we ate the crackling and the juicy bits off the beef and all the rest of it: everyone ate everything, in fact. And I distinctly remember having pork or beef dripping sandwiches – 'bread and scrape', as it was known – with a little salt for extra flavour.

So we were getting a high fat and carbohydrate content as well as plenty of protein and vegetables. But the diet did us no harm because everyone was always on the go, and all our activity simply burned it off again. We didn't eat snacks between meals, like people do now, and we had very few sweets or biscuits. Cakes came out only when there were special visitors, which was all to the good.

Gardening was my number one activity, and if I had to choose between that and anything else it would always take first place, although at the time it was the end result – the money – that really appealed to me. I thoroughly enjoyed doing it, but it was never an all-year-round occupation: from October through to the end of March I was at school during the hours of daylight, so there was almost half the year to do other things.

In the summer it was different and there was plenty to do on the plot, but even on a Friday evening I could get my allotment jobs done and still be out by about nine o'clock to enjoy myself. I'd do the paper round first, and then go up to the allotment to dig the potatoes and pick the beans. I was very serious about earning money. When you came from a background where you had little and had to work hard to get anything, you appreciated it when you got it and didn't mind the hard graft it involved.

Even though I was busy, I made sure there was always time to go out, especially in the winter when the evenings were too dark to work outside. You had to be eighteen to belong to a club, so almost until the time I left school pubs and working men's clubs were not a part of my world, although my mother actually worked as a cleaner in one of the clubs and my father was a member.

Our Welsh coffee bars

THE MAIN GATHERING PLACE for youngsters in the sixties was the *bracchi*, the name given in Wales to the Italian cafés that sprang up everywhere early in the twentieth century as immigrant families came and settled here. The Contis, Sedolis, Franchis, Strinatis and the Bracchi brothers, who gave the cafés their generic name, made them popular meeting places well before the war years, when many Italians were persecuted or interned as aliens and possible collaborators (Churchill had famously said 'Collar the lot!' after Mussolini entered the war), even though lots of Italians in the valleys were first- or second-generation Welsh by then.

There must have been six or seven *bracchis* in Tonypandy alone. There would be a shop at the front selling sweets loose from tall jars, and cooked meats and bread to take out, but they were mainly rooms →

where people went to eat and drink – no alcohol, only coffee or tea.

Older people would call in there on a shopping day for an inexpensive lunch, all home-cooked, but they didn't tend to go there in the evenings. On Sunday evenings especially the *bracchis* became meeting places for us youngsters, somewhere warm and dry that wasn't expensive for a cup of coffee or a soggy pie heated up under the steam. And you could make a coffee last several hours while you talked.

On a Friday and Saturday night we generally went dancing in Tonypandy. There were two main places, Judge's Hall and the Library Dance Hall, which were both alcohol-free and just served soft drinks and crisps while we danced to live groups. The Library was at the Miners' Welfare, where they had snooker tables and a good library on the lower level, and then upstairs a huge sprung dance floor and a big stage where they would generally have a seven- or eight-piece band. The Judge's Hall tended to have smaller four-piece groups rather than a large outfit.

Tonyrefail, where I now live, was the place to be in the sixties, once I was eighteen and allowed to drink alcohol, because it had a nightclub called Meadowvale, where they used to bring up-and-coming groups or bands from outside the area. You'd read about them in the paper, and then they would actually appear here in the early part of their career or when they were on the way down again.

Even the various boys' clubs used to run dances regularly, although they tended to have records rather than live music.

The working men's clubs would usually have a drummer and organist up the front for 'proper' dancing – foxtrots, waltzes and quicksteps. Every club had its own dance hall built on, each with a bar, lounge and a 'Big Room', as they called it, where they would have bingo first and then a session of dancing. On Saturdays they didn't generally have much dancing, and they would put in more tables to pack the members in, but in the week and on Sunday nights there'd be ballroom dancing.

As a teenager I was naturally more interested in rock and roll. I went through the teddy boy stage, complete with drainpipe trousers, sneakers and long jacket (although I never had the string tie), and fluorescent socks too: red, yellow, pink and I don't know what. And there was the obligatory curl in the middle of your forehead. Later I got caught up in the Beatles era, when I had long straight hair. You just get drawn into it all, don't you?

Round the valleys the big name in the mid-sixties was Tommy Scott and the Senators, the group everybody wanted to see. They were wild, and I was in Llwynypia one Saturday night when they were paid off because they were too noisy, interfering with the men sitting quietly and playing cards. That was before Tommy Scott had his big break and became known to everyone as Tom Jones.

So there was quite a lively social scene in the valleys and, despite the long hours of hard work, I went out regularly to enjoy myself with my mates. That was when my income from the allotment came in handy. I'd put a lot of hours in, but then I didn't have to worry where the money was coming from to buy the coffee or milk shakes, a bottle of pop or a bag of crisps.

As my teenage years passed, I was working harder and harder at school. I had sat my Eleven Plus exam at

Pontrhondda Primary, which was about three-quarters of a mile from where I lived and so within easy walking distance, and passed that to go on to the local grammar school when I was eleven years old. In the two Rhondda valleys there were four grammar schools and the same number of secondary modern schools, where you went to do practical subjects if you didn't pass the Eleven Plus, so there were eight senior schools in the area, all within the space of four or five miles.

Schools weren't very large in those days and simply served the immediate locality, and the biggest senior school would have about 300 students, perhaps a maximum of 400. Primary or junior schools weren't as big, because they were really local, and the nursery schools were smaller still – even now the one I went to when I was two and a half is just one building, no more than it was in 1949. They were all council schools and you just went along to the nearest.

There was a kind of pecking order among the grammar schools, even though they were in different locations. Porth was considered the highest, Tonypandy (where I went) the second best, Treorchy third and Ferndale fourth, but they were all good in those days and would attract the brightest graduates as teachers.

I remember there was a strong bias towards rugby at all of them, and this was compulsory unless you were actually in a plaster cast: a cold or anything else like that didn't excuse you from turning out on the wet rugby pitches on PE days, in hail, snow or sleet. Football was unheard of at the grammar schools; it was all 'oval ball' stuff in the winter and then cricket and athletics in the summer.

I really liked school. It was not a place I dreaded going to, and I think I enjoyed learning. I suppose I must have been reasonably bright academically, too, because I was in the 'A' stream and went on to pass nine GCE 'O' levels (you either passed or failed each exam then, and didn't have grades). I did all the usual academic subjects – including sciences and Latin – and then went on to the sixth form to work for chemistry, physics and maths at 'A' level.

My aim was to go to university to do chemistry, the other love in my life, although I hadn't a clue what I wanted to do with it: teaching probably, because my brother was a teacher and I never really thought about other options. A large number of grammar school students from the valley seemed inevitably to land up in teaching, and the area was recognized as a big exporter of teachers.

At school there was never any career instruction, nobody ever gave you choices, and so you drifted along in the academic stream almost unconsciously, through 'O' levels and 'A' levels and university, and then finally you got a degree and you had to decide what you were going to do with it. You just cruised down the same old path as everyone else, never dreaming you might hit a brick wall.

In 1964, when my 'A' level results came through and I hadn't passed chemistry, I was devastated. It had always been my best subject, and in my mock exams and everything before that I had done extremely well. My father put in for a re-mark, but that didn't change anything, so I must have had a complete mental blank on the day.

Now I was in the wilderness, because I'd never planned for anything other than university. Although I didn't realize it at the time, failing the examination was in many ways a blessing in disguise, because if I'd gone away to study my allotment business would have collapsed, a possibility I'd never considered. I had been accepted for Cardiff University, not that far away, but I couldn't have come back every week and the allotments would almost certainly have suffered. When I came back afterwards as a graduate I would probably have been in a totally different frame of mind.

In practical terms the result made little immediate difference. I still had my allotment empire to look after, I could carry on living at home, and I went back to 'Pandy Grammar in the autumn to retry chemistry. But the shock of failing the exam had jolted me awake, the students I was with were not the friends I'd had all through school, and spending a whole year repeating work seemed a huge waste of time. After about six weeks, I decided I didn't want to do that.

My father said, 'Well, what *are* you going to do then?'

I said, 'I dunno' – a typical teenager's reply, it seems to me now.

Someone we knew was a lecturer at Treforest Polytechnic, as it was then, and he told me there was a vacancy on their Dip. Tech. course in chemical engineering. It hadn't yet started and I'd be eligible to join it with my two 'A' levels. But my heart wasn't in that either and, although I gave it a go, I very soon left again to look for a job. The vacancy at the pencil factory didn't seem an obvious choice, but they were looking for a chemist and, as I was still keen on the subject, I applied in November, went down for an interview and that was that: I started straight in at their laboratory.

Royal Sovereign, as they were called, were a well-established, family-run company and quite a large concern, producing very high-class pencils that were distinctively branded in red with a gold tip. They were suppliers to the Queen, so they bore the royal warrant as well.

At that time industrial standards and regulations were beginning to focus on hazards like lead in the paint that coated pencils. Children used a lot of pencils, and often chewed them as well, so the company needed a chemist to check that everything was 100 per cent safe.

My routine job was to test all incoming materials, using the kind of chemistry I had studied for my 'A' level. When materials such as paint were delivered, I simply took a sample back to the laboratory and went through a range of tests to eliminate the chance of anything nasty being in the consignment.

But another, more fascinating part of the job was in effect quality control. There were masses and masses of formulae for a host of different types of pencil, and I was expected to go down on to the shop floor, work with the people involved in the different manufacturing processes, weigh out the various ingredients and evaluate them, and then do quality checks all along the line as the product was being made.

Possibly nothing looks quite as humdrum as the commonplace black-leaded HB pencils that we all use at some time for making notes or drawing, and as a gardener I used them regularly without giving them a second thought. I certainly didn't realize until I joined the pencil factory that there were hundreds of other kinds: cosmetic pencils such as lip-liners, eye-liners and eyebrow pencils for Max Factor, Outdoor Girl, Revlon and all the other main cosmetic companies. There were oval red carpenters' pencils, fat stumpy black ballot pencils, 'chinagraph' pencils for writing on glass and under water, and 450 different shades of coloured pencils – there could be something like 25 shades of green alone. And there was the full range of hardnesses from 6B to 6H in the standard black-leaded pencil.

All the pencils were treated in the same basic way, whether they were cosmetics, colours or leads. They all depended on critical quantities of ingredients, the graphite in the lead pencils and the pigments that needed precise weighing to produce the various shades of colour. At the end of the process, samples of the final batches were brought to the lab for me to check that everything was right before they were shipped.

I soon discovered a 'lead' pencil wasn't actually made of lead – one of the potentially dangerous substances, along with arsenic and antimony, that I was constantly on the alert for – but of graphite, a natural form of carbon that's lustrous and very soft. To make it hard enough to use, the graphite is mixed with china clay, and the proportions of these two main ingredients determine the hardness of the pencil.

When the factory made up a particular order for pencils there could be 1 cwt (50 kg) or more of 'lead' to mix first, and I had to be there with the guy on the shop floor to supervise the weighing of ingredients in huge scales and to make sure they were in the right ratio. They were then transferred with a controlled amount of water to a large rotating drum of pebbles that helped grind and blend the ingredients for a specified number of days. It was rather like a sophisticated version of mixing concrete.

Once the fine slurry was judged to be right, it was pumped out, filtered and dried, and sent through the 'waltzer', a machine like an old-fashioned washing mangle, with enormous stainless-steel rollers that crushed the slab into a really fine powder. This was mixed with water once more and then pressed through holes in a die to extrude the long thin threads that you could recognize at last as pencil leads.

These were forced out on to long boards with shallow grooves cut in them, then they travelled past girls who rolled them by hand to make sure they were completely round and cut them up roughly to length. They were then baked dry for several days in the hot room before going to the chopping room, where they were cut to the exact length of the pencil, which might be any shape and description.

All this long process was needed just to produce the lead or 'slip', as the internal part of a pencil is known in the trade.

From the slip factory the leads went over to the wood-working plant to be turned into proper pencils. Canadian pine came in as flat, solid pieces that were cut into slats, each the right size to make six or seven pencils. These were 'thick-nessed' and grooved, the leads were automatically fed in, glue was spread on the surface, another slat would come out on top, and they were clamped to dry as several pencils in a rectangular block. Once the block was dry, other machines shaped the hexagonal, round or oval profile of the pencils and then cut them individually from the block.

The whole process often took weeks, and yet once everything was up and running the factory could turn out finished pencils at the rate of a couple of hundred gross an hour (quantities in the pencil business are always multiples of a gross, or 144).

Then the pencils had to be painted. The paint coat was built up from several films of cellulose lacquer only microns thick, the number depending on the quality of the pencil: an average could be four or five, but a top-class pencil would have anything up to ten coats, each followed by a long journey down a conveyor belt to allow time for it to dry.

Even then a pencil wasn't finished, and still needed to be given its distinctive livery or cap, and to be printed with the grade and brand. A pencil's decoration was important for sales and identification, and could be quite elaborate. Staedtler, who eventually took over the company, produced black-and-red-striped pencils with a little black and white crown at the top end, while the more upmarket Norris brand had yellow and black stripes topped with a crown, the colour of which varied according to the hardness of the lead.

I found all this out after I had been with Royal Sovereign as a chemist for a year, when the management decided they also wanted an engineer who understood the various processes. So they sent me back to college on day-release to do an ONC in production and mechanical engineering. I did well in that and went on to do an HNC, all the while working my way round the different manufacturing stages on the shop floor.

Finally they bought out a company in London who specialized in making the extra-small pencils for diaries. These had plastic caps on the end to make sure they didn't fall out and get lost. The machine that made them duly arrived, and then they said, 'Right, now what do we do with it?' So I was given the task of learning all about injection moulding, setting up the machine and making all the diary caps.

I found it all fascinating and more than just a job, but the pressures were becoming ridiculous. I was at college two nights and one full day every week and studying to get my qualifications. Everybody was on bonus at the pencil factory, where there were rigid targets because large amounts of other people's money were at risk if things weren't running well.

My allotment business was in full swing and occupying much of my spare time, not that I minded having to go up there so often. Far from it: at the end of a shift in the pencil factory I could hardly wait to get home and cast off my working clothes, impregnated with the distinctive smell of the factory. I'd change into my old homely things and go along to the allotment with a sense of relief and anticipation.

It was great to breathe in the fresh air once more and admire the familiar surroundings. The allotment changed so much with every season, especially when its brown lifeless appearance over winter gave way to hope and expectation as the first promising green shoots of spring started to appear.

And I'd got myself a girlfriend. I went out with my group of friends one Saturday night (8 April 1967, as Anthea always reminds me), and we ended up in the National Union of Miners' club in Tonypandy. I was sitting there, drinking and chatting and reading my *Football Echo*, when two young brunettes, one of them tall and slim, came walking towards our table. They asked if the two seats at the end were taken, we all quickly said no, and they duly sat down. Very soon I noticed that Tudor John, one of my friends, was deep in conversation with the taller girl.

'You've clicked there all right,' I congratulated him.

'No,' he said, 'she lives next door to me!'

He and I swapped seats. Now, in those days any entertainment in the clubs was usually preceded by a few rounds of bingo. And I said to Anthea (although I didn't even know her name at that stage), 'Will you mark my bingo ticket for me while I finish reading my *Echo*?'

She gave me a strange look, probably thinking that was the worst chat-up line she'd ever heard, but did as I asked. As usual we won nothing. The game ended, I offered both girls a drink, and they replied in unison that they'd each have a vodka and orange, at which I nearly fell off my seat: I wasn't used to buying anything other than beer, which was very cheap in the clubs in those days.

We chatted occasionally during the show, and at the end I offered to walk her home. Before we parted we agreed to go out together the next night.

'Where shall we meet?' I asked.

'On Pandy Square,' she said. This was a popular meeting place for young people from the area.

'No need to walk down there,' I said, 'I'll pick you up at the end of the street.'

'Oh . . . you've got a car!' she said, quite taken aback, because this was exceptional among youngsters in the valleys during the sixties. I mentally thanked God for the results of all my hard work on the allotments.

So we met again that Sunday night, she got in the car, and I had to admit straight away that I couldn't remember her name.

'Anthea,' she replied. 'And you're Walter, I presume?'

'No. I'm Terry,' I said.

'But all your friends were calling you Walt.'

'That's my nickname,' I explained.

After that stumbling start we were on our way.

I drove us to the Vale Country Club, some twelve miles from where we lived. During the evening various friends started arriving until, by eleven o'clock, the place was packed. Then the lights dimmed, the curtains at the side of the room opened, and out came this young lady in a robe with a tape deck – there were no fancy sound systems then. She also had with her a large laundry basket.

The music started and she removed her robe, revealing that she was somewhat scantily clothed. She began to dance around the floor and then opened the basket, drawing out an enormous snake, which she draped round her neck as she gyrated to the beat of the music.

The look on Anthea's face is imprinted on my memory to this day. I apologized profusely, but we still remained there until late. By the time I got her home it was 2am: her father was standing on the doorstep, arms folded and looking menacing. I dropped her off and quickly asked when I could see her again.

'Next weekend,' she replied before going in to face the music.

Despite that embarrassing beginning of our relationship, we were engaged in July 1967 and got married a year later, on 20 July 1968 at St Andrew's Church in Tonypandy.

Wedding flowers

AT 5.30 ON THE MORNING of our wedding I was up at the allotment. Several days before, Anthea had decided she wanted yellow roses for her bouquet and her bridesmaids would carry posies of sweet peas. So there I was on that pivotal day in my life, cutting all these flowers, which had to be perfect. I picked the very best, some of the loveliest blooms I have ever grown, and took them to the florist in Tonypandy who regularly bought her flowers from me. She had to make up these arrangements and deliver them to Anthea's parents' house by mid-morning.

I then went back home and got myself ready to meet up with my best man, John, and walk to the church a mile away in time for the wedding.

When Anthea came through the church doors with her bridesmaids, all carrying their beautiful floral arrangements, I could feel a lump in my throat as I thought how I'd been able to supply these special flowers for this special day, from my own allotments. Plus a touch of professional pride that, just like the vegetables I sold to my customers, they were only a few hours old!

Before that important day, the Royal Sovereign pencil factory was taken over by Staedtler, another famous name in the industry. All the original family members were replaced by a new management team sent from Germany, and this meant a complete change for us.

One day I fell out with the new management. I was trying to get a job finished in the polishing shop when the new second in command came and wanted the tea machine sorted out. At the time it didn't make sense to me that I was busy on an important production process and yet he was insisting I stop what I was doing simply to fix a tea machine.

This was in the summer of 1968. Anthea and I had got married in July, shortly after the factory shut down for the annual holiday, and we hadn't been back long. My whole life had changed: we were living with my mother- and father-in-law, we had recently signed up for a new house that was being built, I was about to go back to college in September to finish the last year of my HNC course, and I was working with a new management team with a different way of doing things.

And that day I just blew my top and told them to stick their job.

Terry's Tip for May

French climbers
AS AN ALTERNATIVE to runner beans, especially on exposed sites, try growing some climbing varieties of French beans, which may prove more successful as well as often coming into bearing earlier. Climbing French beans give a heavier yield from a smaller space than their dwarf counterparts,

which have never been popular on our damp hillside because slugs can reach up and nibble the ends of the pods, while the heavy Welsh rains tend to make them dirty.

Runners need bees to pollinate them, and in wet windy conditions there is often a heavy drop of flowers that can cover the base of the plants with a rich red carpet. French beans, on the other hand, are self-pollinating and so every flower will form a bean, and even though they don't bloom as prolifically as runners the eventual crop is often heavier.

There are two main types of French bean varieties: those with broad flattened pods and those with round fleshy pods, which I prefer because they tend to be less stringy when mature and seem to freeze better. When I first tried climbing French beans I grew a variety called 'Hunter', which cropped extremely well, hung a long time on the plant without going tough, and was slow to run to seed.

The pods are flat, however, and not as popular in our household as the fleshier round kinds, and so I changed to 'Cobra', a top-class round variety with all the qualities you'd expect. They're so good that many other allotment members have been converted to this variety.

Anthea's Recipe for May

Gooseberry Fool
(900w microwave method)

*A*S SPRING TURNS *to summer, gooseberries start to swell up and look promising. Although still hard and green, they can be used for cooking, and picking the biggest thins the rest of the crop, leaving the remaining berries about 2–3 in (5–8 cm) apart to make good-size dessert fruits when they become fully ripe. The thinnings are ideal for this recipe.*

* **1 lb (450 g) gooseberries, topped and tailed**
* **2 tbsp water**
* **3 tsp cornflour**
* **¼ pint (150 ml) milk**
* **1 egg, beaten**
* **¼ pint (150 ml) double cream**
* **4 tbsp sugar**

Put gooseberries and water in a large microwave-safe bowl and cover with clingfilm, leaving a slight gap at one side. Microwave on high for 6 mins, stirring every 2 mins.

Leave to stand for 5 mins. Then press the fruit through a sieve to remove pips and make a smooth purée.

Blend cornflour and milk in a small dish, microwave on high for 1 min, stir, and then continue cooking until visibly thickened. Beat well after cooking.

Add the hot sauce to the purée and stir in the beaten egg. Put aside and leave to cool.

Whip cream and sugar in a basin until thick, and then gently fold with a metal spoon into the cool fruit mixture. Spoon the fool into 4–6 sundae dishes and refrigerate for 2 hours before serving.

CHAPTER SIX

Settling Down

I WASN'T THROWN OUT OF the pencil factory straight away. After my thoughtless outburst I was dragged over to the office, where they basically told me to leave if I wasn't happy. By then I had calmed down and said, 'Well, it was just a heat of the moment thing,' hoping everything might blow over.

But it was too late, and the production manager said, 'No, we can't have this kind of attitude here. As soon as you find another job, you're out.'

So I had to go home and break the news to Anthea, not many weeks after getting married and committing ourselves to the new house, which was going to cost us all of £3,500, a huge amount in those days of single-figure weekly wages.

I was glad then that I still had my vegetable empire going strong. An allotment plot can be different things to different people, but as I was discovering it is also many things to the same person. For me it had meant land where I could do what I loved most and where I could earn good money relatively easily, supplying produce that people around me needed and enjoyed. It was sound exercise in the fresh air in congenial company. And now it proved to be almost a consolation and a reassuring kind of continuity.

Fortunately Anthea was well aware of my passion for the allotments and the amount of time and commitment they took out of our life together. She accepted that right from the start, and all through our marriage has happily shared me with that plot of land on a Rhondda hillside.

And I had the car, which I soon found made transport a lot easier and quicker. It had brought other benefits in the days before I got married. I was the only one among my friends who owned a vehicle, for example, so it became popular as a means for us all to travel further afield to dances.

We could venture beyond the valleys at weekends, especially in the evenings when we started exploring places such as the very trendy (to us then, at least) Vale Country Club, the place where I took Anthea on our first date. This appealed to us because it provided gambling facilities – poker, blackjack and roulette – quite lacking in our district.

Adventure on the road

OWNING A CAR ALLOWED me to go with two of my closest friends, Dai Martin and John Rees (my former fellow allotmenteer and entrepreneur), on camping holidays outside Wales. Before we went away I'd usually go to the allotments and collect vegetables to sustain us during our week's camping. I'd take a whole sack of potatoes because chips were our staple diet for the week, and since there was insufficient room in the boot this paper sack, together with some of our other possessions, was usually kept on the roof rack.

I remember one night we couldn't find a camp site and so we parked up in a lay-by, on a hill outside Southend. It was raining heavily when the three of us settled down to sleep in the car.

In the early hours of the morning we were woken by a steady bumping on the car roof and bonnet. We sat for a few minutes summoning up the courage to go and confront whatever was out there, and finally agreed that on the count of three we'd all leap out together.

When we did we found that the mysterious intruder was the paper sack on the roof, which had split open in the wet and was allowing potatoes to drop out and roll off the roof on to the bonnet, and down the hill towards Southend. There went our food supply for the week.

The empire really flourished once I'd got wheels. Now I could deliver in luxury and easily pick up extra potatoes whenever I ran out, and I carried on unabated during the four years I was at the pencil factory, running the business on the ten allotments and selling all the produce at the weekends.

I can't pretend it was easy, because in those days we

worked long hours – 7.30 until 5.00 from Monday to Friday, plus Saturday mornings from 7.30 till 12.00 – which meant the allotment business was concentrated into Friday evenings after I came home from work, with all the deliveries fitted into Saturday afternoons. Sundays I spent up there working the ground as usual.

We had a Mountfield tiller by then to help with all the cultivation. My father had decided it would be a good idea to invest in this 3½ horsepower (2.6 kW) machine, which made work a bit quicker, if not necessarily any easier. The trouble was that the paths and the narrowness of many plots meant you couldn't really till across the slope of the mountain: for ease you had to till up and down. But all the plots sloped steeply and so, going up, the machine tended to bury itself in the ground, and when you came down you were usually running to keep up with it.

In addition most of the plots on our site are not square but more like a trapezium, some short and wide and others long and narrow. All measured the standard ten perch in area, but with different shapes. Cultivating some of them wasn't too bad, but because my ten plots were scattered I had a variety of shapes, some of which were never easy to turn over. And, as with all machinery, the thing wouldn't always start on the days I wanted to do something, and I'd be pulling and pulling at the starter trying to awaken some sign of life, and then I would open the choke and flood the engine. That often meant spending an hour or so stripping it down and cleaning everything out, just to get it going. So I could easily waste an hour before I'd even started. The fact that I would always rather dig by hand anyway didn't help matters.

Using the tiller would have been much more practical if the plots had been laid out on a large flat area. But, as always, the contours of the valley affected what we could do up there. For example, some of the plots run by other people have been terraced, divided by permanent paths and edged all round with 'zincs' (corrugated galvanized-iron strips) to create a series of plateaux down the slope, but that's not something that appeals to me.

My allotments did have the edges neatly finished off with zincs, but each plot was a single undivided expanse. And I had no permanent paths within a plot, just one on either side, as now, with another at the bottom where my blackberries grow and an access path to the front of the greenhouse.

All the rest I trod out on the soil wherever I needed them, and then dug them in again at the end of the season. I think this method wastes less ground than the currently fashionable network of permanent paths and small beds. I've always tried to get the maximum possible yield from a plot, and I feel my kind of layout favours this.

Another way of ensuring a good yield is to double-crop at least half of the ground, arranging sowings and plantings so that an early batch is followed by something else as soon as it finishes. You can't do that with some vegetables, which occupy the ground for so long that there isn't the time left in the season to follow with anything useful. But my basic repertoire of early potatoes, fast small carrots and early cabbages or broad beans was always cleared with enough time to fill the space with a follow-on batch of lettuce, radish or something quick like that.

I was still avoiding winter crops. The days were too short to cultivate them after work, and going out in the soaking wet and trying to dig parsnips or pick sprouts in a stiff north-east wind never really appealed to me. Meeting any demand would have been difficult, because even with ten plots on the go I couldn't guarantee a complete basket of veg for a normal dinner in winter.

Nor could I have risked interruptions when people expected a steady supply. My kind of gardening wasn't an occupation where you could miss an occasional weekend, simply because the weather was too harsh for you to gather the produce. If you make commitments, you've got to meet them and make sure the orders are filled.

This was part of the challenge in summer, meeting an order when I had run out. It was never possible to make up the shortfall by buying from one of the other gardeners: I never bought beans or potatoes or anything else off any other plotholder. Some grew for their own purposes and wouldn't have a surplus to sell, while a few of the others did sell a bit, but then only to certain customers. It was generally accepted that they had their clients, I had mine. There weren't that many members on site by that time anyway. I had ten plots at my peak, Tommy Parr had a good handful and the top was more or less empty, so between the two of us we must have had more than half the plots that were in use.

It was four or five months before my next job (my *other* one, because I've only ever had two in my entire working life), and the growing season was well and truly over when I finally left the pencil factory in December 1968, four years to the month since starting there.

I was to remain with my new employer for thirty-three years (a whole generation) until I retired in 2001. And in the process I worked up from one of the original dozen employees to managing director.

Like so many famous companies, Perkin-Elmer started life in simple, almost primitive conditions. Richard Perkin was the inventive partner, a New York astronomer who found in the

1930s that he couldn't buy the kind of telescope he needed to carry on his work, and began making them himself in a garage in a New York suburb. People soon discovered these telescopes were very good and wanted to buy them, so he started a small business making and selling optical instruments.

After the Second World War he realized that the chemical industry was developing fast and lacked precise instrumentation to check the quality of chemical products quickly. To meet this need he invented the first infra-red spectrometer, a big heavy beast of a machine that would shine light through a particular substance or cell. By doing various calculations you could then analyse what this substance was from the results, using reference graphs supplied with the machine.

At this point Charles Elmer, a rich financier, came on the scene. He recognized the potential of these analytical instruments in industry, with the result that Perkin-Elmer was founded as a partnership in the late forties. It took off immediately and grew at a phenomenal rate. By the mid-fifties they had opened their first British sales office in Beaconsfield, Buckinghamshire, and very shortly afterwards started up a factory there to produce instruments for the European market.

The company was making lots of money and investing much of it in research and development, so they were soon offering more sophisticated analytical methods – first infra-red and gas chromatography, then ultraviolet and nuclear magnetic resonance – and quickly established a complete range of instrumentation, which was assembled and tested at their Beaconsfield plant. But in the late sixties they began to have problems in finding sources to supply the small volumes of high-quality components they wanted.

About that time south Wales was becoming a big regional development area, with large incentives to draw companies in to fill the voids left by the decline of heavy industries such as coal mining and steel. Perkin-Elmer were offered an attractive deal to open a factory in Llantrisant, and this was started up in early 1969 to make essential components for shipping up the motorway to Beaconsfield.

We started here with a machine shop and sheet metal shop of just 20,000 sq ft (1,846 sq m), which is small by industrial standards. But with the demand for instruments growing so large and so quickly Beaconsfield soon ran out of capacity, and we built another 30,000 sq ft (2,770 sq m) to make their gas chromatographs for them. In the early seventies more production was moved to south Wales. Then we set up an electronics plant making circuit boards and harnesses because more and more electronics were being built into instruments. Very shortly afterwards we added another 60,000 sq ft (5,538 sq m) of factory.

Then, in the early eighties, we hit a slump, and a large section of the factory stood empty. Beaconsfield was still building instruments, but in an ageing ex-munitions factory. There was a plan to knock it down and redevelop it, which we were afraid might mean everything moving up there. But the Americans said no, it was too costly and we had space standing idle down here. In the end they closed Beaconsfield and moved all production to Llantrisant. Very few of the existing staff transferred to south Wales, so all the new opportunities and promotions came the way of people already living here.

Back in 1968, when the Welsh chapter of the Perkin-Elmer story opened, I'd been told to leave the pencil factory as soon as I could, but I wasn't in a hurry and they weren't pushing me: even though I had technically been fired, there was a kind of truce between us.

One day I went along to the Labour Exchange in Talbot

Green, where I found an advertisement on the board about vacancies at Perkin-Elmer and the new factory on Llantrisant Common. I rang them up, and they wrote back to say they were interested.

'Can you come up to London for an interview?' they asked.

London! That seemed a world away. In those days the M4 motorway wasn't open much beyond the Severn bridge between Wales and England. It was 150 miles to London and I had never driven my canary yellow Ford that far in my life. In any case I decided I really didn't want to spend my days making test tubes, which was all 'scientific instruments' meant to me at the time – my laboratory work at the pencil factory had basically involved watch glasses, Bunsen burners, retort stands, simple chemicals and little else. I didn't know anything more complex even existed.

I made up my mind I didn't want to go, and rang to say I was suffering from the flu. About four days later another letter arrived, telling me they had rearranged the interview for another date. I still had several irons in the fire with other companies, so I wasn't too desperate for the job, but I didn't feel I could cancel again and decided I'd just have to drive all that way after all.

The night before the journey I sat down and planned my route with military precision to make sure I got there in good time for the interview: to a valley boy like me, London was a million miles away. I didn't sleep at all well the night before. I was up hours before I needed to be and set off very early, worried whether my little yellow car would actually be up to the long journey.

All my planning paid off though, and I arrived with plenty of time to spare, feeling very pleased with myself. As I drove into Beaconsfield, I remember being impressed by all the huge houses surrounded by their great expanses of ground. No need for an allotment here, I thought: you could grow all you wanted in the garden.

As I realized later, the factory was over twenty miles short of London, so I didn't make the big city after all!

I walked into the factory and met Ken Walker (later to become my first boss), who invited me to have a look round and see what they made. My eyes must have opened as large as gobstoppers! There was this super-clean production area and brilliant lighting, and everywhere strange high-tech equipment and instruments that were far more sophisticated than anything I had expected or could have imagined. It was like something out of science fiction.

We finally sat down together and did the interview, at the end of which Ken told me the job was mine. All the preparation, anxiety and long drive had been worthwhile, and I returned home feeling much happier, pleased with my day's efforts and looking forward to this new career.

And so Boxing Day (which wasn't a holiday then: all you got off was Christmas Day) found me standing on the platform at Bridgend station at six o'clock in the morning, waiting to catch a train up to Reading where I was to get a bus to Beaconsfield. Anthea was all teary-eyed because we'd only been married in July, this was our first Christmas together, and I was going away for two weeks' induction and training. That first New Year of our marriage I spent in lodgings in London Road, High Wycombe.

We duly opened up in Llantrisant on 6 January 1969. There were just twelve of us, the twelve apostles as we called ourselves, all on exactly the same wages: the guys to run the machine and sheet metal shops, an overall manager, and myself as production planner. The idea was that Beaconsfield would tell me what they wanted, and I'd order the materials and the tooling, and plan everything on the shop floor to meet their demand.

We had sparkling, brand new machinery and equipment, all paid for by the development grant, and the government gave the company an extra £4 per week for each of us as part of the employment deal. And from that simple beginning the company grew and grew, until at its peak we employed 275 people.

I started there on £1,000 a year, my first four-figure salary. After all my initial apprehension I had the job and the wage I wanted, enough for us to live on comfortably and to pay for our new house. We were still lodging with my parents-in-law up in Llwynypia while our house in Tonyrefail was being built, which in those days took a year from the time they put in the foundations until everything was finished and ready for us.

We finally moved into our own house in October 1969, and have lived here ever since.

What we liked about our new home was that it was part of an extremely small estate of four semi-detached buildings and three detached houses. The gardens were reasonably large, which immediately appealed to me. All the people who moved in at the same time as we did were young couples, and it says a lot about the stability of life in the valley that four of the original couples are still here, while four more of the properties have had the same residents for twenty years, including Marilyn and Clive, who live in the other half of our semi.

So nothing much has changed since we first moved into our little corner of Tonyrefail, a friendly, secure area where our children have grown up with those of our neighbours. The estate itself has grown over the years to several hundred houses, whose owners are constantly changing, but time seems to pass by our end.

At first our new garden was an extension to my allotments, somewhere extra for growing vegetables. But I soon realized that with all the plots in production there wasn't really any need for this additional capacity. Instead I planted apple trees, raspberries and blackcurrants, and gradually converted the rest to a real flower garden, a place that would look pretty with bulbs, polyanthus, wallflowers and forget-me-nots in spring, followed by a stunning display of bright annuals all summer.

I've always felt the home garden is the best place to cultivate the various herbs used in the kitchen. Certainly in our household wanting a herb is a spur-of-the-moment thing: whenever Anthea prepares a dish, she has all the produce there fresh from the allotment, but at the last minute she'll decide if something's missing from the flavour. This is where herbs always come in handy, but it's no good if they're growing back in the allotment. You need to be able to pop out into the garden on an impulse and gather them at point of use, so always make a corner available for your favourite kinds among the flowers.

Homes were going up everywhere when ours was being built. Even though many people were moving to areas outside the valley with more employment and less distance to travel to work, there was a huge demand for new housing here. The valleys were actually starting to experience a new industrial revolution following the collapse of traditional employment.

About the time I was moving to my new job, for example, the Royal Mint had just transferred from Tower Hill in London to a new plant next door to Perkin-Elmer's factory. It was a standing joke at work that we never managed to finish the tunnel – in fact we had a grinding shop in one corner of the factory, right next to the Mint, and whenever we were entertaining visitors I'd say that I would have shown them our secret had I been allowed to, and that the machine we were looking at could be moved aside to expose a tunnel between us and next door.

The Mint employed a thousand people once it was up and running in its new premises, so it was a huge asset to the valley, and Frams, who made oil and air filters for the growing car industry, employed another thousand. The three factories were the only ones there at that time, but within a few years there were thirty-two different companies on our industrial estate.

It was largely due to the regional development grants available that new businesses were being attracted into the area in the late sixties and early seventies. Electronics companies and big television names like Sony, Panasonic and Hitachi were moving in because they could get huge amounts of capital investment paid for, together with subsidies towards labour costs and a suspension of rent and rates for the first three years after a factory opened. It was an extremely good deal all round.

These new employers needed staff with very different skills from those used in mining and heavy engineering, so it wasn't easy for the out-of-work colliers in the district to retrain. There were some who managed it, mainly younger people, but above a certain age you were rooted deep in a different culture if you had been working down the pit. There you worked hard at the coalfaces, always as a team with everyone dependent on one another, whereas in a factory you are often working on your own with someone breathing down your neck all the time.

Understandably the older miners didn't want to know, and sadly a lot of them never found work again after the pits closed. But there was another generation coming along, the younger element that industry and production always tended to favour because they could be trained to suit the requirements of the job.

Many employers brought their key skilled workers with

them: the Japanese companies, for example, were run by all-Japanese management teams, but they would recruit the rest of their staff locally. German companies similarly, and there were a number of these investing in the area – Bosch set up a factory that made alternators, and Borg Warner manufactured transmission systems.

A lot of the incoming industries offered new opportunities for women and the amount of female employment grew phenomenally. Factories making televisions took on large numbers because the sets were valve-based in those days, with large printed circuit boards, and it was women who assembled them. Simple purpose-made connectors were not yet commonplace, so televisions needed lots of wiring and cable harnesses, all produced by female labour.

A strange result of all this new employment was a kind of unofficial demarcation between different jobs, which took a long time later to break down again. A factory tended to be planned around the assumption that men worked on the heavy machinery or as sheet metal workers and that sort of thing, on the shop floor, whereas electronics assembly-line work and office jobs were taken up totally by women.

You were trained to suit the needs of the particular trade, barriers were seldom crossed, and jobs became stereotyped. Boys came in as shop-floor apprentices and girls became secretaries or trainees in work that required dexterity. Porth Textiles opened up a new factory making Christmas trimmings, and that was almost entirely staffed by women. It was a time of great changes in work attitudes that would persist throughout the next decades.

For me the decade of the sixties closed with one door slamming and another opening up on a completely new world. I soon found that the people I was starting to work for were gentlemen:

Perkin and Elmer ran the company like a family, and their influence cascaded from the top right down to the shop floor.

Everybody knew everyone else's first name and even the standard of dress was unusually high, as if the top quality and high cost of the instruments we produced spread a kind of stimulating influence throughout the company. The senior staff were all high calibre, too, and I often used to reckon there were more doctors per square inch at Perkin-Elmer than in most general hospitals, because they all had PhDs and were clever scientific men.

So starting there wasn't a change that I regretted, and in the end I had twenty-nine fantastic years with the firm.

But, like everything else in life, nothing stays the same for ever, and the last four years were far from happy. We were eventually sold to a company with no appreciation of scientific instruments, and then it all started to go wrong. The new management changed from making components to a policy of buying everything in, which led to the wholesale dismantling of the company.

First I had to sell the machine shop to one company, then the sheet metal shop to another, and the electronic assembly plant to someone else. I came under increasing pressure to do less and less in-house, and buy in larger quantities made else-where for assembly: the management were looking at Chinese, Indian and the burgeoning East European suppliers for components because they seemed to be cheaper.

From 275 employees the labour force fell to just 90, and I felt I was spending half my time calling people into the office and laying them off. All the fun went out of the job, and I heaved a sigh of relief when I finally left there and was able to concentrate once more on my allotment plots, where I knew I could find lasting contentment and continuity.

Terry's Tip for June

Summer lettuces

THROUGHOUT THE HOT summer months salads are an important element of most people's daily fare, and lettuce one of the main ingredients. All lettuce varieties grow fairly fast, given enough warmth and water, but they can bolt to flower and seed quickly in a hot summer, especially if allowed to go dry.

I manage (usually!) to maintain an unbroken succession by sowing little and often, generally two main types: a cos, for its unrivalled texture and food value, and a red-leaved type to add colour to the salad bowl.

Sow the seeds of these in cell trays, those seed trays which are divided into nine separate compartments: this helps avoid pricking out the seedlings as well as root disturbance at transplanting time, both of which can check growth. Remember lettuce seed does not germinate well at high temperatures, so keep the trays in cool shade in a hot season.

As soon as the seedlings emerge, sow another batch to follow on. Transplant the young plants outdoors when they are large enough, and you should find you have a succession of lettuce without any waste (most gardeners grow too many that mature all at once) and some left over to give to fellow plotholders.

Anthea's Recipe for June

Courgette Loaf

OURGETTES (OR ZUCCHINI) are strange plants. Their large seeds make robust seedlings that quickly fatten into lush plants, which then seem to take ages to produce more than the odd fruit, like a miniature green, yellow, white or striped marrow. And then suddenly you have too many, all ripening in quick succession and almost becoming an embarrassment in the kitchen. That's the time to make this delicious fruit 'bread', to eat fresh or freeze for later.

Quantities make 1 loaf
- **1½ cups plain wholemeal flour**
- **½ tsp cinnamon**
- **½ tsp baking soda**
- **¼ tsp baking powder**
- **½ cup honey**
- **1 egg (beaten)**
- **½ cup vegetable oil**
- **1 tsp vanilla extract**
- **1 cup grated raw courgette, unpeeled**
- **chopped nuts, raisins to taste**

Preheat the oven to 175°C/325°F/gas mark 3.

Combine flour, cinnamon, baking soda and baking powder in a mixing bowl.

Add honey, oil, beaten egg, vanilla and courgettes, and blend all together with a mixer or fork.

Add nuts and/or raisins, and blend again.

Pour into a greased and lined 8–9 in (20–23 cm) loaf tin.

Bake for 1 hour. Test by inserting a sharp knife, which should come out clean. Turn out on to a wire rack to cool.

Eat within 3–4 days – on its own, spread with butter, or hot with custard.

CHAPTER SEVEN

Major Changes

THERE'S A REASSURING SENSE of permanence at the heart of life in the Rhondda, echoing perhaps the hard, ancient rocks underlying the valley itself. The family home, the allotments, the locality generally always seemed constant when I was young and gave everything a feeling of stability, even though superficially things might appear to change.

My parents never moved from the house where I was born. My father died in 1977 when he was sixty-eight, still relatively young, but my mother lived on there. My aunt and uncle died and my cousin and his wife returned to live at the family home. They bought the house in the late seventies and my mother lived with them until her own death at the age of eighty-eight. My cousin and his wife live there to this day.

I found there was the same kind of continuity in my

market gardening business, where demand didn't change much before the end of the sixties, and members still grew the same stuff on their plots. I don't think it's necessarily a case of being unadventurous as gardeners, but as a rule what you see growing next to you is a strong influence and you tend to follow suit. There weren't really any pioneers or revolutionaries on the allotment plots; no one came in with radically new vegetables.

Valley character

IN MANY RESPECTS the Rhondda is a very insular society. People have a long tradition of staying put, and even those who come back from living away don't tend to bring new customs and ideas with them. If you did a straw poll of the inhabitants of the valleys, you'd find most have lived there all their lives, as did the generation before *and* the one before that.

It's not like a major city or suburb where people from overseas tend to congregate, taking on allotments to grow the food of their native countries and creating a new demand in shops. There are very few ethnic groups in the valleys. You might see programmes and magazine articles about allotments in Birmingham or London, featuring a wide variety of crops because there are so many nationalities and gardening cultures there, but we don't get that in the valleys.

Books and magazines and innovations from outside the valley don't have that much influence. It's only proof of the pudding which induces people to change here. Every now and then somebody might introduce something new on the plots, like I started using rye grass as a winter green manure, and now there are a couple of other people who can see the benefits and are trying it for themselves. It's nothing dramatic, though.

Change on our allotments is a gradual process, in many cases introduced by default. From time to time people bring in surplus plants they've grown. Allotmenteers are a thrifty race and will usually accept them, whatever they are – waste not, want not. In that way we were introduced to kohl rabi, aubergines, artichokes and many more novel crops. When these were harvested they were passed around for other plotholders to adopt if they liked them. Who said allotment gardeners have no sense of adventure?

Wales has always been very much a sheep-farming country and, apart from Pembroke and their renowned early potato tradition, there was nowhere that produced market garden crops in commercial quantities, and no farm shops to stock new vegetables for people to try, so most people either grew their own basic crops or were content to buy whatever was on offer. The range of choice in greengrocers and even in the first supermarkets hadn't really evolved in the early 1970s, small, local shops tended to supply what the customers wanted, and there wasn't the diversity of fresh food we see today. People didn't travel much or explore new ways.

Few of us could predict the radical changes that were just round the corner.

There had been the long war years and then the rather grey fifties, with poverty and rationing and normal life apparently a long way off. And then suddenly in the late sixties everything began to explode. The growth in new industry developed an enormous momentum, the structure of the family began to change significantly as wives became an important part of the work community, and everyday life changed for ever.

The decline of coal mining was the major catalyst. As a pit closed down it would be replaced by a large estate of light industries, like Creeds, who made teleprinters, British Airways, Aero zips and various clothing companies such as Polikoff's, which is now Burberry. There were a couple of large heavy engineering firms, but many men travelled out of the immediate area, to Treforest or Bridgend and their large industrial estates, while much of the local work was now for women.

Prosperity began to increase as households now had two breadwinners instead of just one, with more disposable income, and this affected the traditional pattern of family life. When both parents were out at work children had to be farmed out to grandparents or became latchkey kids, often from an early age, and so were left unsupervised, free to do whatever they wanted.

And with the extra income that two wage-earners could bring in, the need to grow your own began to decline. People didn't want to come home from work and then go out digging an allotment or growing vegetables: why bother when you could afford to go to a shop and buy it?

Throughout the seventies the allotments were pretty quiet. We were losing members and only a small handful of people were really interested. Enforcing the rules became pointless, and there was no way you would evict anyone because soon you'd have nobody left. The tradition of cultivating a whole allotment was ignored, and often people would come in and tend just a couple of bits, enough to keep themselves going, and not worry about the rest of the plot.

It was a real depression from the point of view of people's attitudes towards allotment gardening, and not just on our site. The valleys once had lots of allotments – they seemed to be everywhere you went – but complete sites began to disappear before your eyes.

Over in Pont Rhondda, for example, there was a huge established site alongside the railway line, and that's where they built the Rhondda College – the whole of the allotments went suddenly to make way for the college buildings. There's a good allotment site in Trealaw that has survived, but on the other side of the valley, opposite the cemetery, a big site disappeared to make way for a new cottage-type hospital.

Whole chunks of allotment land were vanishing at a rapid rate wherever plots were not being used or were falling derelict. Up and down the valley the demise of allotments was reminiscent of the decline of the coal industry and the constant pit closures.

As tenancies dwindled on our own site, the shrinking number of stalwarts left began to fear their long association with their plots might soon be lost altogether. Not that the staunch hard core was that easily dismayed: after years of coping with the vagaries of everything Mother Nature might throw at us, we weren't prepared to give up easily. Our slogan could have been 'We shall not be moved'!

We were always under threat anyway because of the local geography. A big council-house estate had been built to one side of us, and an existing estate on the other side had been expanded. We sat in the middle and were always afraid the council would try to combine these two estates. Ours might be a statutory site, but once plots become vacant that status doesn't count for much, and there was a serious worry at the time that the allotments might go to allow a road to be built along the mountain to link the estates.

Nonetheless the letter from the council dropped through my letterbox one morning like a bolt from the blue. I feared the worst immediately, but still felt shell-shocked as I read the enclosed notice of termination on our agreement. I passed the news on to the rest of the members, and gloom settled like a large cloud over the allotments.

The situation needed a measured approach, so I got in touch with our contact at the council, who allayed some of my fears by explaining they actually rented the site from a local farmer, and it was he who had terminated the agreement over some dispute with them. All was not in fact lost, and they were applying for a compulsory purchase order for the land. We were to sit tight!

So we all carried on as normal, in a kind of rent wilderness, for three years while the wrangling about the compulsory purchase went on over our heads. Eventually the council bought the site as agricultural land and all threat of building on it disappeared. That left a group of very happy and relieved plotholders, not least myself: the equilibrium in my life had been restored and I could now carry on gardening there for as long as I was able to draw breath.

With those two estates flanking us, we might have expected an increase in our numbers, but the people who tended to move in there were younger or had been relocated, and they weren't really interested. There wasn't even an influx from residents without much of a garden – perhaps one here and there, to give it a try, but they certainly didn't reverse the downward trend.

I was still in there with my ten plots and loyal customers, but revolution was in the air at home as much as in the valleys generally. What with getting married in 1968 and starting at Perkin-Elmer the same year, I realized the new decade was going to bring different pressures into my life.

It was no longer just me and my vegetable empire; now life started to revolve around the responsibilities of a new wife, new home and new job. It's the kind of adjustment many young men have to make, not always easily. Anthea was familiar with my gardening activities before we got married, and knew exactly what I was doing. Fortunately she was quite happy to come up to the allotments and be there with me, not to garden – that would have infringed the old male-only bias – but to keep me company while I did various jobs.

Something Anthea and I always disagreed about was my total disregard for the state of my paths. My argument was that I had enough to do keeping the plot weed-free without worrying about the paths, and anyway you couldn't grow anything on them. So whenever she came up there she'd put me to shame and set to, making an excellent job of tidying up.

Anthea also reckons I give her all the back-breaking jobs of harvesting the fruit from the gooseberries and blackcurrants. This isn't so! All I ever said was, 'You want the fruit, so I'll grow it and you harvest it.' And then there's the fiddly chore of tying sweet peas, which regularly prompts her to chide me: 'You only bring me up here so I can do the jobs you hate.'

Anthea's main gardening responsibilities lie at home, where she looks after the ever-changing flower scene in our front and back gardens. We have very few permanent plants and prefer to change with the seasons, with spring bedding like bulbs, wallflowers and forget-me-nots being replaced by gaudy annuals in the summer. She also has the onerous task of watering the hanging baskets and tubs that adorn every spare inch of the gardens.

But she enjoys her frequent visits to the allotments and is now a bona fide member of Albie's coffee club (reasonable fees – just bring the occasional jar of coffee and powdered milk; water supplied free, but *not* from the large blue water butts, which are reserved for washing the cups).

Right from the start Anthea supported me in my regular Friday night and Saturday morning routine of making up and delivering vegetable orders, not least because at that time it was still a good source of income.

At first we were still living with her parents and being fed at home by her mother, but once we moved into our new house I suddenly had to think about providing food for our kitchen. We were now two independent people, and almost overnight I went from following a simple four-month routine during which I grew, gathered and sold everything, to trying to provide food for most of the year to keep the larder full. I even had to contemplate winter vegetables for the first time!

My father was still there, growing veg on his two plots and keeping an eye on mine: he'd be up every single day of the week, working or sitting there with his cold tea and sandwiches. If something needed attention on my plots he wasn't beyond just going over and doing whatever was required. The sowing I tended to do myself, but anything else like watering and general maintenance he'd do for me, and there was never a rigid demarcation line. It was like an insurance policy really, because if anything was wrong he would let me know as soon as I got home.

The trouble was that 'home' now meant a drive to the allotments whenever I wanted to do any work. In those days (there's a bypass now) the journey involved travelling through the various villages, which were becoming more and more congested, and in practical terms I was now a good half-hour away.

I'd drive up through Tonyrefail itself, then through Penygraig, and then drop down through Tonypandy, which was the main shopping centre and extremely busy at week-ends: people didn't go off to supermarkets then, and did all their shopping in 'Pandy on a Friday or a Saturday. So I had to get through there, and then go on up through Llwynypia itself before I reached the plots.

And the journey was getting steadily worse. Because of the way houses are packed tightly into the valleys, there are no car-parking spaces, forecourts or garages, so everyone parks on the main road. As a result of the prosperity reaching the valley in the 1970s, husbands increasingly owned a car, together with their wives and perhaps one of the children, so parking was more and more difficult, the streets ever narrower. It wasn't by any means a quick drive, despite being only five miles.

The extra journey time probably wasn't as large a factor as the other changes in my life, because I still wanted to go there, however long it took. It is good to visit your plot every day for many reasons. How much time you then spend there will depend on what you want to do and how long you can spare, but when you get there you might as well take your wristwatch off because time means nothing.

There's never any point gardening and watching the time, because you can't plan properly, and one job leads to another. I always find while driving there that my mind's preoccupied with a few tasks I need to tackle on arrival. What a waste of brain power! When I get there some job I hadn't planned for usually sticks out like a sore thumb and so I get on with that instead. Then, as I look round, other tasks catch my eye. The moral of this is not to waste time and energy planning work in a garden: what needs doing will be obvious as soon as you look at it.

By itself the distance was never a real disincentive. I enjoyed being there too much and it was my major source of relaxation, an opportunity to unwind and a real tonic after working all day in a factory. Although I was lucky enough to have an office with windows and could at least see what the weather was like, there was still this pane of glass between me and the fresh air. On the factory floor itself it was all artificial lighting, you never caught a glimpse of the outside world, and I couldn't wait to get back out in the open air, to take a good deep breath once more and see what was going on in the 'real world'.

The best time on the plot was always early July, when everything was in its full glory. I would look forward to that, and still do. As you walk through the potato plots the plants all sport the delicate colours of their flowers, indicating they'll soon be ready to harvest. By then the rows of runner beans are covered with their bright crimson blooms, creating a magnificent flowering hedge.

In the weeks before that, especially in late May, the runner beans are starting their quest to reach the top of their canes. There are always some that have lost their way, the ends of their long shoots flapping vainly in the breeze. I gently wrap these back round their supports, like helping a child to walk for the first time (but take care when you do this: a runner bean climbs in an anticlockwise direction, so don't confuse it by twining it the wrong way!).

Thinning overcrowded seedlings is always an important task, but in late spring it needs to be done promptly to ensure robust healthy crops. You always tend to sow small seeds too thickly, and successful germination can result in a host of congested seedlings. Spread the thinning over several visits, just in case you lose any casualties to pests, and that way you'll end up with a full row of strong plants that can look after themselves. Leave them overcrowded for too long and they'll perish!

Without any doubt the sight and scent that excite all my senses in late spring and early summer are always the long rows of sweet peas in full bloom, their colours glowing in the evening light and their fragrance overwhelming me with a lasting, almost hypnotic effect. You don't necessarily have to go along to your allotment to work: it can be deeply satisfying at times just to look and admire the results of your labours.

Another new pressure was the amount of time I needed to spend at home. There seemed to be an increasing number of chores to do around the house when I came in from work. When we moved in it was an empty shell (unlike today when you can move into a fully equipped home), and there were just the two of us living there at first. In those days you never bought anything until you could afford it, so there were plenty of do-it-yourself jobs that needed doing, all things that took time.

But it was a bit of an adventure really, making a home in a new house. We had parquet floors throughout the downstairs and no carpet, so we collected odd bits of rug. Parents helped out with a television, we managed to buy a three-piece suite, and at least we had a bed in our bedroom, with some cheap MFI wardrobes to keep a few clothes in. As we put a little money away we gradually improved things here and there, and were steadily getting on our feet.

When we had been in the house only two years and were still in our early twenties, it pulled us up short when we found out Anthea was expecting our first child, who was born in 1971, bringing real change into our lives.

I remember the occasion very well. It was one of those balmy May days when I had just come home from work. Anthea was hot and bothered, and in the last stage of her pregnancy. She looked tired and said, 'Do you have to go to the allotments this evening?'

'No,' I replied. 'I'll tell you what: sit down, I'll get some food together, and we'll go to the seaside for the evening where it'll feel cooler.'

We were sitting there on the seafront, enjoying the picnic, when Anthea said, 'I think I've started labour.'

This was our first time, I was a complete novice and knew nothing about childbirth, and I thought we'd better get back to collect her things and go to the hospital. We arrived in plenty of time, and I sat in the room holding Anthea's hand and trying to be the perfect reassuring husband. Then the doctor came in and said, 'Would you go outside now, Mr Walton.'

So I did and, thinking everything was under control, naively went straight back home!

It wasn't long before I had a call demanding, 'Where are you? Get back here quickly.' After a long night, during the late morning this rather bonny lad was born: our first son, Anthony.

The arrival of a first child is a major event that every couple has to adjust to in their own way. For me it meant extra pressure on the simple way of life I had been used to. Soon I found I was getting up at 6.30 in the morning to start work an hour later, getting home at night and immediately dashing to the allotments for an hour or so, and then coming back to my evening meal just in time to see Anthony briefly before he went to bed.

Then in 1974 our other son, Andrew, was born.

This time we knew what we were doing, and Anthea made sure I didn't leave the hospital. Once more it was an all-night affair, and I stayed with her almost until Andrew arrived (in those days fathers weren't welcome at the actual birth).

Now our family was complete, with our two sons, one very dark and the other very blond. They turned out to be wonderful sons and great brothers, always sharing and looking out for each other in a crisis. Although they're not yet hooked on allotment life with all its pleasures, I can detect early signs of them coming round to following in the Walton tradition.

At first the allotments helped me to keep everything in perspective. There was no point my coming home from work and then staying in the house, because I'd be touchy, and I think Anthea appreciated that the nights I came in and stayed in I was more hindrance than help. I couldn't switch easily from one enclosed environment to another, and felt I didn't want to talk to anybody or hear the phone ring or have to sort out problems. There had been enough of that for eight or nine hours at work.

I was in a sedentary occupation, not doing anything physically active in the factory. My job there was to work at a desk and come up with plans, and although I wasn't on my feet and working hard like a craftsman or labourer on the shop floor, at the end of the day I still felt exhausted with all this pent-up energy, and needed somewhere to go out and do something physical. The allotments provided that, a lot more cheaply than going to the gym, and it was in the open air. I thoroughly enjoyed working up there, even in the winter months.

So everyone was better off if I went there for an hour or so and came back afterwards feeling refreshed. Anthea was tired, but I'd be ready then to look after the children and give her a break, have a meal, sit down and enjoy a couple of hours' relaxation with her before going to bed.

By then Anthea had given up her job as manageress of the shoe department in our local cooperative. That was a very responsible position, and at the start of our marriage she was earning more than I was, so I felt I needed my allotment income just to keep up with her.

We agreed soon after Anthony's birth that she would stay home and bring him up, because we both believed that stability in a child's early life is paramount. I was fortunate in having a good job with excellent prospects, but it was a demanding one. And there were the allotments too, which meant that I would not be around to help out as much as I could wish. Anthea remained at home until the children were in their early teens, before finding a part-time job that allowed her to get them off to school and be at home when they returned.

This approach was not unusual in valley life in those days, and mothers with young children tended to be at home in large numbers, which wasn't as bad as it might sound to modern ears. There were plenty of opportunities for them to meet up during the day and socialize, helping each other out and having coffee together. There were no lonely days while the men were away at work.

We both discovered the arrangement actually enhanced family life. I found it helped relieve the pressure on my various activities, and I was able to organize very enjoyable and rewarding leisure time to spend with all three of them. I made sure, too, that I always took my full four weeks' leave so that we could go away for at least two holidays a year, maybe only to Tenby in a caravan or somewhere local, but it was a break.

Just after Anthony was born, Keith Harris (who I suspected

later of winding me up over the BBC phone calls) joined Perkin-Elmer and came to work for me in production control. We got on well together: he had the same sort of character as me, and a family of almost identical ages to mine. The factory in those days was a very sociable place, organizing children's parties and activities for families, and we always seemed to be together when we went to the various functions. Eventually our families would go on holiday together, often to a Pontin's holiday camp.

One year we went to a camp in Brixham, run by an ex-Royal Navy lifeboat man known as DAC. Although he ran this holiday camp for families, for some reason he was always grumpy with children. If any of them went to play pool he'd make them put a couple of pence in the lifeboat charity box, and if they wanted anything he'd moan and groan about 'kids again'.

After a couple of days of this we'd had enough, and we started going from there over to Pontin's nearby for the entertainment. The girls used to be terrified, but Keith and I would just drive through the gate, park up and walk in as if we belonged there. And when we went back for our nightcap we used to wind up DAC in the bar every night.

We finished our week there and came home, but I kept on wondering if I could get some fun out of the situation. I knew that the mother of one of the guys at work lived in Brixham. So I concocted some headed paper with the name of the camp and the full address, and wrote a letter that said, 'It's part of camp policy that every month we run a draw of all the people who stay here, and the winning name receives a free holiday with their family at the expense of the camp whenever they want it.'

I sent this letter to my contact in Brixham, and she posted

149

it back to Keith Harris. Nothing was said for a bit, and I began to wonder what had happened.

Finally he rang me up and said, 'You'll never believe it. I've won a holiday at DAC's down in Brixham.'

'Have you?' I said.

'Was it you?' he went on.

'Why, where did the letter come from?' I asked him.

'It was posted in Torquay,' he said.

I said, 'I've been working with you, and I haven't been on holiday since I came back with you. So there's no way I could have been in Torquay to post it.'

'Oh. Well, I don't know what to do. The kids hated it.'

I said, 'Well, you could stay there like we did last time. It's a free base, there's no cost or anything, and you can go out and enjoy the area round about.'

A week later I had another phone call and there was Keith on line, fuming.

'It was you!' he said. 'I rang up that place on Sunday afternoon, and DAC picked the phone up. He'd obviously been asleep and I woke him up. I said I was ringing up about my free holiday. "What free holiday?" he said. "We don't give free holidays here." I told him I'd got this letter, and he said, "Somebody's winding you up!" I knew it must be you then.'

That was just one of many such incidents. We continued to go away together as families, to Yugoslavia and all over Europe, and we're very good friends to this day.

After Anthony came along and I found it more difficult to arrive home and just disappear, I considered reducing the number of plots I was looking after. I was still running ten of them, but I felt my standards were dropping, even though (like everyone else at the time) I was using all the relatively inorganic fertilizers and insecticides. They seemed to be a boon because they were less labour-intensive than organic methods: all you did was open a packet or blast things with a spray. And my emphasis had changed, now that I wanted to grow crops all the year round so as to eat off the plot for as long as I could.

I didn't shed them all at once. The plot with all the roses on was ready to go anyway, because I hadn't replaced the plants over the years. They were starting to go woody, and the quantity and quality of the flowers were declining. Like everything else, plants have only got a certain lifetime, even roses. You can prune them hard back but eventually they age and begin to deteriorate. So I decided to give them up altogether.

At that stage I still had my customers. Most of them had stayed with me all the way through and they would take whatever I had. In most cases they didn't even place an order and would just tell me to bring anything I had to offer. This made it easier to offset things – if one vegetable was a bit short, I simply took something else to make up the order, which was great, and they would eat whatever I gave them. It was almost a forerunner of the vegetable box schemes that are popular now: you get what's in season or at its peak. Nothing's new in this world really, and the wheel continues to turn, every few years returning to its starting point.

When I had started some fifteen years earlier, my customers had tended to be older people in their fifties and sixties who were happy to eat vegetables every day – unlike many of the younger people now living in the valleys, the double-income generation who wanted faster food and often didn't eat the meat-and-two-veg-with-gravy type of meal. Younger people were starting to look at rice or pasta dishes, egg and chips, and things in packets or tins.

And the daily meal wasn't central to family life any more. People didn't sit down together: they simply went and cooked something quickly or opened a packet and sat in front of the television while they ate. The dining room as a key gathering place was going out of fashion.

Although my old customers meant a lot to me, there was no way I could continue the business as before, and as I began to abandon plots I had less produce available. Gradually I stopped delivering. Many of my elderly customers relied on this home delivery for their supply of good wholesome vegetables, so I felt great sorrow over letting them down. But I simply couldn't carry on what was becoming a frantic lifestyle, and still do justice to my family and my work. By the mid-1970s, if people wanted anything they would come up to the allotments and collect it. And over a four- or five-year period I reduced the number of plots from ten to two.

Before I could finish running them down, my father had a serious heart attack.

This was a major shock to everybody as he was a big guy, always active and considered to be extremely fit. When he came to Wales from the Midlands he had driven a concrete mixer on building sites, working on the new Aberthaw power station and then locally on housing developments. At the rear of our house in Church Street they built a large council estate of a hundred-odd houses, and his last job was there, quite close to our back gate and the old childhood route leading to our mountain playground.

He would visit his allotment 365 days of the year, usually after he'd finished work, and very rarely took a holiday. And when he was up there he spent a long time on his plots because he always found plenty to keep him busy.

Then, right out of the blue, he had this heart attack and was in Llwynypia Hospital for five or six weeks. In those days they didn't know much about treating heart attacks and the usual regime was just bed rest. When he came out, his life seemed to have ended. He now lacked the confidence to go up to the allotments in case he collapsed again, and would get out of bed every morning and just sit there, his mind still gardening even though his body wasn't.

I used to drive past the house every day on my way to the allotments, so I'd always call in for a cup of tea with my mother and father, and he would give me a long list of instructions, without having seen what was happening on the plots. He'd say, 'Don't forget now to put these lettuce in and sow these beetroot. Do this and do that. And by the way, don't forget to tie up something else.'

He had no idea what was actually going on up there. So I just used to nod and say, 'Yes, all right.' And then I'd go up and do whatever was necessary, based entirely on my own judgement.

It made a big impact on me, his not being up there any more. On a Friday when I was busy he used to go and get a few potatoes or pick the beans and prepare some of the stuff for me, so that when I came home I could do the heavier work and then box up the vegetables and deliver them. He was always there to help out with things. It was a strange relationship really because, although I looked upon the plots as my empire, I think he did the same, as if they were his. We never quarrelled or argued about things, so there was never any problem. It was always just 'ours'.

Even after he became ill he carried on trying to help run the business. He'd suddenly say, 'Mrs Williams wants 2 lb of beans, Mrs Evans wants 2 lb, and Mrs Jones wants 1 lb of beans.'

And I'd say, 'Dad, I'm not picking yet.'

'Well, why not?'

'Because they're a bit late this year, that's why.'

'You must have put them in too late, then.'

It was always my fault!

This went on for about two years. Then, while I was away working in Brighton for Perkin-Elmer, I had a phone call from my brother to say Dad had got out of bed during the night, collapsed and died.

That seemed to change life completely. For two years he had not been up there in person, keeping an eye on things every day and doing jobs round the plots to help out. But now my mentor of the allotments over all those years, my teacher right from the age of four, had gone altogether.

My mam was more devastated than anyone by the suddenness of my father's departure. She was always the quiet rock supporting her family of three men, all standing six feet tall and towering over this lady of only five foot six. We believed we were the mainstays of the family, but it could never have functioned without her.

She had always worked hard, never complaining about her lot in life, and kept us going with plenty of good solid food prepared with a meagre budget – we never went short, and there was always a generous dose of love thrown in for good measure. She became an expert at turning all the vegetables we grew into interesting dishes! My brother, Eric, and I owe her a huge debt for the way she brought us up and guided us into happy lives.

Mam remained in the same house close to the allotments after my father's death, taking an active interest in everything that went on there and visiting my plot on many occasions, a thing she had rarely done during my father's days: the changes taking place in this once male-dominated world affected even her. And she lived on in very good health, with a plentiful supply of fresh vegetables from the allotments, for fifteen years after the passing of my father.

When he died in 1977 I was already down to three plots. Now all I wanted to keep were his own original plots, which were more important to me than all the others put together because they were part of the family tradition. I wanted those two to carry on and not fall behind, so I gave them preference, gradually shedding the rest.

Those two plots suited me down to the ground because he had built sheds and a greenhouse on them, which I didn't have on my old plots. I'd never bothered because there was never any need: I kept my tools in his shed, and he would raise any seeds in his greenhouse, where he was growing tomatoes and starting other plants that needed protection.

Two plots seemed enough for me then. I had no customers any more, but I was providing my brother and my mother with vegetables, and we ourselves were eating all the year round from there, including the children. Right from the time they began on solid food they had vegetables from the allotment, not preserves from a shop in jars and tins. Anthea used to take whatever was in season and liquidize it, so they were introduced to fresh seasonal food at a very early age.

Looking back, I wonder if that gave the boys the taste for home-grown vegetables. While they were small they used to join me on my plots but were much more interested in playing games than gardening, and neither showed the same passion at an early age for allotment growing as I did. But now both of them have a yearning to grow things, particularly Andrew, who grows all his plants from seed to fill his pots, baskets and borders. Lately he has taken on a small piece of land to grow vegetables, so perhaps at last some of the latent gardening genes are coming to the fore.

About the time my father went out of my life, Tommy Parr, my other great influence, gave up – his health was going and he couldn't garden any more. His son Ray took over his plots, reducing them to two just as I had with mine. The big difference was that, whereas my father had left me to work out things for myself, Tommy was the keenest of showmen and a perfectionist. So when Ray came up to help him, Tommy supervised him closely and never let him think things out independently.

I remember one instance when Ray was planting potatoes. Tommy grew lots of potatoes for exhibition, with a number of different varieties, and when you show a sample it has to be all the same variety. Ray was steadily planting these tubers and had reached about three-quarters of the way along the row when he ran out. So he sensibly started on the next variety.

As he was filling in the trench, Tommy came up and said, 'Why have you started using that box there?'

'Well, there wasn't enough to fill the row,' Ray explained.

Tommy was furious. 'Get them all up! Now! We can't have mixed potatoes in a row.'

And Ray had to dig up the whole row of tubers and throw them away. With memories like that, it was no wonder he was never really happy working Tommy's old plots. Eventually he gave them up.

I kept my father's two plots going until about 1992, when I moved to the single plot where I am now, quite close to the gate. Joe Vickery had tended it for years, so it was in exceptionally good condition. There was a large 16 x 8 ft (5 x 2.4 m) greenhouse already on it, and I made a little wooden shed. Then Anthea's father died in the same year, and he had just put up a new shed in his garden. I thought there was little point letting that pristine shed go to waste, so I moved it on to my plot, and it's still there giving good service.

Joe's gooseberry bush

JOE VICKERY MUST HAVE planted my solitary gooseberry bush, a green variety with a reddish tinge and at least twenty years old by now. It's a real phenomenon and completely abused, because I've never really looked after it since taking over from Joe. It just sits there at the top corner of the plot, where my trailerloads of manure are tipped and left until I have a chance to barrow the stuff down.

This possibly excessive feeding is all the attention it gets, and must suit it because it regularly throws 30–40 lb (14–18 kg) of fruit each summer, even on our exposed hillside. Only exceptionally severe conditions will discourage a gooseberry because it is one of the toughest fruits, weathering most winters unscathed. The winter of 2005/6 was particularly hard though, the coldest for at least ten years, and a persistent run of cold easterly winds scorched some of the branches and growth buds, reducing the amount of blossom and fruit.

I've never really pruned the bush or kept the centre open – there's even ancient lichen growing up the main stem. It might not be what textbooks advise, but I've tended to leave it alone because it was doing what it had to do, producing lots of fruit. Other members see the crop on it and think it's fantastic, so now its offspring are growing all over the allotments here. I don't take cuttings: the weight of the fruit bends some of the branches down to the soil where they actually form roots, and I just chop these off and give them away.

Tommy Parr was secretary of the allotments committee when he decided to give up. That year we had the AGM, and Tommy told everyone it was going to be his last year. The other committee members said to me, 'Well, you're the longest-serving member, you've always been involved in all the procedures. Will you do it?'

I said yes, all right, but I felt that we should be sharing the job round the different members so I said I would take over just for a couple of years until everything settled down. That was in 1977 and I'm still doing it now, because nobody else wants to take on the responsibility.

So the seventies was a decade of change all round, both in the life of the valleys and in my own circumstances. I had a growing career, an expanding factory, a new house, a wife and two children. My market garden empire of ten allotments had shrunk to just two plots, I was now secretary of the committee, and neither my father nor Tommy was there any more with words of wisdom to guide and help me. I had had to alter my ways radically.

Terry's Tip for July

The protection racket

AFTER YEARS OF GROWING crops with artificial fertilizers and chemical sprays I went almost completely organic, and soon found this can raise problems because pests don't always recognize the fact and cooperate with you. They see all those luscious and vulnerable vegetables as their next meal, and it can take several years to rebuild the numbers of natural predators to help keep the pests at bay.

Don't despair! The easiest way to deter them without resorting to potentially deadly chemicals is to intercept them with protective covers and barriers, especially in high summer when so many are on the wing or migrating round the plot on foot. If you study the enemies' behaviour carefully you can usually think of simple but effective ways to stop their game.

Make a cage from wire or bamboo canes over your brassicas and sheet this over with fine mesh or fleece to prevent the cabbage white butterfly from laying its 'eggs in a cluster, yellow as a duster' underneath the leaves. Simply draping fleece over the plants as a 'floating mulch' can work just as well: it's very light-weight stuff and the plants will push it up as they grow. Erecting fleece 'corrals' round your carrots (see p. 201) will protect them from being decimated by the carrot root fly, which cruises around near the soil looking for choice sites to lay its eggs.

Anthea's Recipe for July

Gooseberry Chutney

*A*S GOOSEBERRIES APPROACH *maturity, you may feel hard put to find appealing ways of using their often very lavish crops. You can make fools, jams, wine and endless pies and tarts with them, and any surplus freezes extremely well. But they are also ideal for making savoury preserves, such as this really simple but almost addictive chutney from Anthea's repertoire.*

* **3 lb (1.35 kg) ripe gooseberries**
* **4 onions**
* **8 oz (225 g) sultanas**
* **1¾ lb (800 g) brown sugar**
* **1½ pints (900 ml) malt vinegar**
* **2 tsp salt**
* **1 tsp turmeric**
* **1 tsp mustard**
* **¼ tsp cayenne pepper**

Top and tail the gooseberries, peel and chop the onions, and put in a large pan.

Add all the other ingredients, bring to the boil and then simmer for 2 hours.

Pour into warm sterilized jars and seal.

CHAPTER EIGHT

Back to My Organic Roots

As a professional chemist I might have been expected to see the light about the lavish use of inorganic materials in the garden much sooner than I did. After all, my main responsibility at the pencil factory had been to analyse raw ingredients for signs of toxicity, so I should have been alert to the more sinister qualities of garden chemicals.

For several years, however, chemical fertilizers and insecticides made gardening so much easier – especially when life was crowded with other activities and time on the plot was strictly limited – that we all used them liberally, without question. We were grateful for their instant benefits. The fact that their effects were cumulative and in the long term poisonous to man and beast took a while to become obvious.

These things had revolutionized gardening. I started my

allotment career organically (although nobody called it by that name), simply because there was no real alternative. All of us used whatever manure and compost we could lay our hands on, in my father's case much of it gathered by me on the mountainside, and that provided our fertility.

Pests could be treated with a few lethal remedies, but were usually tolerated if the attack wasn't serious, or removed by hand when their numbers grew to threatening proportions. Diseases were cured by the simple and time-honoured remedy of culling and burning affected plants – ruthless but effective.

In my empire days I had all the opportunity I could wish for to do things the old way: my commitment was to the allotments, and I didn't owe my time to anybody else. If there was a choice between doing something in the summer months on the plot and going out dancing or for a drink with my mates, then the allotments always had the edge. I had work to do, and there is no way you can mess about with nature and get away with it. When it stays light until half past nine at night, there's still time to go and have a beer later or meet up with mates for an hour or so. But you can't waste a good May evening going to the pub at seven o'clock when there's gardening to do.

Once I started work, however, I didn't have all summer to go out and fetch bracken and manure from the mountainside, nor the time to inspect plants daily for signs of trouble. At the busy seasons of the gardening year I for one was ready to welcome any easy alternative to the traditional laborious methods. And suddenly a panacea for every problem seemed to be available. Along came the now notorious insecticide DDT, a very little of which was guaranteed to kill almost anything that moved on your plants, and lindane, another lethal insecticide that was very efficient but took almost for ever to break down in the soil.

Artificial fertilizers became more common – simple compounds such as sulphate of ammonia or nitrate of soda, and more complex balanced mixtures of feeds, particularly National Growmore – and these quickly made gardening productive and very easy indeed. No more worries about collecting large amounts of humus to feed the soil. Instead you raked in a couple of good handfuls of National Growmore just before sowing or planting. When everything came through, you gave it another boost with a sprinkle of sulphate of ammonia, a sudden fix of nitrogen that made plants spring into life. They'd shoot up green and healthy almost overnight.

As soon as a pest attacked, you came out with a little pack of lindane or DDT, puffed the white powder all over the plants and nuked the pests to death. Every insect in creation was now easily bumped off, crops seemed clean and unblemished, grew extremely fast and looked luscious.

This practice steadily spread during the mid-sixties and into the seventies. It was a revolution. We started to buy these chemicals for the allotment store, everybody began using them and the results were almost instantaneous, partly because we were overdosing everything, giving all our plants quite excessive amounts.

I think that initially no one even considered flavour, because the stuff looked healthy and inviting. After all the toil and care that had gone into raising the crops from seed, fighting off the pests and feeding all that lavish growth, we were almost bound to enjoy the fruits of our labours. It's disconcerting to realize we didn't spot any difference in flavour and eating quality.

By the early seventies I had gone from fully organic to almost completely inorganic on my plots. With ten to look after I had barely enough time to plant, grow and harvest the stuff and then sell it. There is only a short window in April and May when everything must go in, and it seemed to take an inordinate amount of time to get all the crops under way.

And then during late May, June and July the weeds became rampant, mainly because they loved these inorganic feeds as much as did the crops. A handful of sulphate of ammonia makes a cabbage look dark green and extremely appealing, but it does the same for weeds, which seem to leap out of the soil and flourish even more strongly than before. This made more work for me: it was like feeding a lawn when you don't like mowing.

But on the whole it made gardening a lot easier, producing quick results with little effort. All you had to do was spend a pound or two on a 1 cwt (50 kg) sack, which then lived in the corner of your shed. Every so often you took a plastic bucketful and cast it round all the plants while the ground was wet, and within days they would start to look extremely healthy. The more you used, the better they looked. No need to go humping tons of heavy manure any more.

Chemical insecticides, too, seemed the answer to every gardener's prayer, and we didn't appreciate that they were not just destroying the enemy but killing allies as well: anything that moved died. But I don't suppose realizing that would have alarmed us unduly, because we didn't seem to need these friendly creatures now we had a more foolproof method. If this white powder could kill all the pests, who needed ladybirds, hoverflies and those other beneficial insects that were now defunct anyway?

Every advance was greeted with enthusiasm and a regrettable lack of caution, and it wasn't clear for ages that we were creating longer-term problems.

About twelve years after the advent of the chemical revolution on the allotments, however, concern was expressed that these substances were going into the soil, where they were accumulating and doing no good at all. Articles started to appear in gardening magazines about the poisonous side-effects of insecticides on wildlife and the way residues were building up in the bodies of birds and animals, resulting in their declining numbers.

I had been working in industry with chemicals long enough to know that there's never smoke without fire, and when the use of insecticides became a real issue I stopped immediately. I didn't wait for conclusive proof. As soon as there were rumours about their safety I started to think, hold on, I've got two young kids who are eating that food, living on it constantly. So the first thing to go was the use of lindane and DDT.

Then it became evident there was more and more water pollution occurring in local streams and waterways from excessive amounts of nitrates draining from the soil. Again, what was happening everywhere was obvious, once you really thought about it. Chemical fertilizers were concentrated and worked quickly because they were soluble, so that plants could take them up straight away. But if they were easily dissolved it meant that any residues were soon washed out of the soil by rain, and these had to go somewhere.

We knew the effects on the plot were short-lived because it was evident at the beginning of any new gardening season that when plants came up they were struggling. There was no fertility left in the soil, especially in the Rhondda valley, a wet, hilly place where, from late September or October right round to the following March, rain fell constantly on the sloping ground, leaching out these chemicals and carrying them straight down into the river.

By the time this was common knowledge, all of us on the allotments had fallen completely into the habit of using chemical feeds, at first just one or two basic kinds and then the various superphosphates and potashes. Eventually there seemed to be an inorganic fertilizer for any need – potash to feed fruiting plants, superphosphate to help beans to set, nitrogen for quick growth – and all in a scoopful of powder. It was so simple.

Some people made weird and wonderful cocktails with different materials. One of the worst was a mixture of lime and sulphate of ammonia, which causes a chemical reaction that makes your eyes water. It was particularly useful on brassicas to help fight clubroot: even though the ground would have been limed beforehand, adding a bit extra was a good insurance against the clubroot, while the sulphate of ammonia made everything grow fast and green. But when you mixed the two together, the smell of ammonia was tremendous and should have warned us something wasn't right.

Importance of lime

EVERYONE ON THE PLOTS had limed the soil regularly for as long as I could remember, and lime was one of the few ingredients that the early gardeners here actually bought: looking back at the records of sales at the allotment shop in the 1930s I see the only entry in the ledger is for the sale of lime.

Our soil tends towards acid clay and lime is the perfect additive for reducing this acidity, adjusting soil conditions to a pH in the range 6.5 to 7.0, which is near perfection for most of the vegetables we grow. It's the ideal conditioner for improving the structure of our heavy soil, and for adding to ground where you're going to grow brassicas, which it helps protect against clubroot.

I use it regularly to this day, because it's still one of the best and most natural things for improving soil fertility and texture. If it's added on a rotational basis, any part of the plot will be limed every two or three years, so there's no chance of an overdose. Legumes need it as well as brassicas, and even though I manure my bean trench deeply, the surface always gets a very thin coating of lime to sweeten it.

I made a resolution never again to trust anybody's word on something which had been man-made nor to use any form of artificial additive in the garden, even the modified insecticides which were so-called 'safe'. They might have been 'tested' but there is no test that can reliably take into account the really long-term effects. It is the same with herbicides, like the glyphosate we're using everywhere in agriculture: no one can predict the long-term impact of regular use.

Giving up the use of chemicals left me with the problem of what to do instead. In place of herbicides I resorted to the simple alternatives of hoeing or hand-pulling weeds among my plants, and hacking them off my paths on a hot day, leaving them to wither and dry out. Replacing inorganic fertilizers and insecticides was not so straightforward. But I had to find something: intensive cropping needed to be supported with some kind of regular feeding or the soil would eventually become exhausted, and pests would continue to appear and threaten the health of my crops.

I soon discovered that alternative methods of controlling pests aren't in fact hard to find. They all depend on vigilance and a prompt, ruthless response: you have to keep an eye constantly open, and the moment you spot a pest you must counter-attack with every means available.

There are two methods I regularly find very successful. When you first see a pest, use your thumb and forefinger to crush the larger ones individually, or rub your fingers up and down a leaf or stem where a whole colony of something small like black or green flies are feeding. That will usually kill 99 per cent of them.

If an infestation is more severe, I get my hand-held pressure sprayer, fill it with tepid water from one of my drums, pump it up to the maximum pressure and set the spray to a full hard jet. Then I put my hand at the back of the plant to support it and blast the pests off: most don't swim too well, so they tend to drown on the wet ground.

The only pests I've failed with to date are slugs and snails, and I haven't yet completely eliminated the use of the notorious blue mini-pellet. But my usage has dropped dramatically, I avoid exposing wildlife to them, and I don't throw them liberally over plants once these are large enough to look after themselves. But when I start seedlings under a cloche or under fleece I always add a few mini-pellets, because they're isolated there from wildlife and are ready to catch all the slugs and snails that gather in that piece of paradise: plenty of tender food, a lovely warm environment and complete protection from predators.

There are alternatives, like copper deterrents and coarse mulches, but on a full-size allotment these more intimate measures just aren't practical. It's the same with parasitic nematodes, which seek out and feed on baby slugs in the soil. They are difficult and expensive to apply to large areas of ground, and in an area that gets an excessive amount of rain you would be adding them for ever.

Slugs and snails are one of those problems that have to be lived with. We're never going to eliminate their populations, especially on an allotment site backed by a vast expanse of mountainside that's always damp. I suspect they get sick of grazing on the rough pasture up there and decide to charge down in the summer for a good feed, like raiding parties off the hillside. You can almost see the rustling in the grass as word gets round that you've just planted your lettuces.

The other method that I use more often in my own garden involves going out after dark with a large torch and a kitchen knife with a pointed blade. I shine the light into their eyes, and while they are dazzled I hit them with the kitchen knife. This is quick and surgically precise because I know exactly where the heart is! It satisfies the sinister side of me and also amuses the neighbours, who see this moving beam at eleven o'clock at night and catch a glimpse of me in my balaclava, flak jacket and blacked-out face.

I use no pellets whatsoever in my own garden because I don't want to harm the frogs living in my pond. They are good allies, but unfortunately there aren't enough of them to keep all the pests under control. Many years ago we used to have a good population of thrushes, which were extremely efficient at clearing snails, but these days we never see one. I'm sure the general use of slug pellets can't have helped. The birds don't realize a slug or a snail has been poisoned, in the early stages at least, and feeding on them may well have affected their numbers. We really haven't done the creatures we share the planet with any favours over the years by our careless use of all these chemicals.

My rhubarb soup (see p. 182) seems to be effective on brassicas as a combined feed and caterpillar deterrent, but sometimes a butterfly manages to get through and deposit its telltale yellow eggs under the foliage. Just turn over the odd leaf as part of your regular inspection and rub off any egg clusters you find.

If you notice little holes appearing in a brassica leaf, turn it over and you'll probably discover a mass of tiny, recently hatched caterpillars, easily dispatched with your finger and thumb. Even then one or two can escape and you may get caterpillars three-quarters of an inch (2 cm) or so long: don't waste these, just pick them off and throw them in the hedge for the birds.

There are some pests you can't control by organic or chemical means, and possibly the most persistent is the rabbit, a widespread raider wherever gardens and allotments sit next to open country. If you've got rabbits, you've got problems, unless you accept they are always going to be there and protect your garden instead of trying to eliminate them.

We had a question about that once on Jeremy Vine's show. The caller explained that she had just taken on an allotment and rabbits had got in: what could she do? The first inclination of some people would be to shoot them, but I'm not really into that sort of thing and it's certainly not advice that would go down very well on air.

I said, 'Well, rabbits are rabbits, and they will decimate a plot very quickly, given the chance. The trouble is that they browse on the best bits, taking out the centres and ignoring the outer leaves. If they would only eat the outsides and leave the rest alone, you could at least still use things. What I would do is dig a trench all round the boundary, put up a wire netting fence with the bottom part down deep in the ground, and completely enclose the area. That's the only way you'll keep them off your veg.'

We don't sell any chemical insecticides in the allotment shop now, apart from slug pellets. I was already secretary and controlled what we bought at the time I went organic, and I simply never stocked them. I'd say, 'Sorry, but I don't sell those,' without giving any explanation, because I wasn't about to become an evangelist and try to convert people who still favoured them. On the other hand I don't want to use them and it would be completely hypocritical of me to sell them, so I adopted a passive way of trying to discourage the others on the allotments.

We do still sell some inorganic fertilizers, such as Growmore and sulphate of ammonia, because many members still depend on them, and I don't think their sensible use has the same alarming effect on the environment: it's over-application that does so much damage. But over the years there has been a decline in their sales, and we sell a lot more blood, fish and bone, for example, than we do Growmore.

Again I try to persuade people by my actions. Apart from all the manure and compost I collect over the year (of which more anon), I buy one bag of blood, fish and bone and one bag of concentrated fertilizer based on cow manure, and I mix them half and half to make a surface feed that I scatter around growing plants on a rainy day to give them a bit of a boost. I rake in the same mix as a top dressing before sowing or planting. The concentrated manure is a quick source of the plant nutrients needed for growth, while the blood, fish and bone gradually breaks down to give a slow-release feed over the longer term.

Whatever method you use, whether it's organic or inorganic, I find you always need to keep an eye on fertility on an allotment. Food crops are intensive, greedy plants and you've got to feed them in some way, basically spend a bit of money to accumulate. It's no good just sticking plants in, hoping the ground is good enough for them to grow well. You might get away with it the first year, perhaps, but the second year you certainly wouldn't.

After a winter in the ground most chemical feeds are all gone, so you start out every spring with virtually infertile soil, and even organic fertilizers are quickly lost from the ground. When you work in humus and natural compost and manure over a period, however, you build up the soil with slow-release nutrients as well as improving its texture, making it easier to work.

The problem for many people is finding enough manure and other bulky stuff, especially in town where you may be far from stables and farmyards. I make a lot of compost on the plot from green waste materials, and supplement this with manure, which I collect regularly during the summer months (not the winter when it's wet, heavy and unpleasant to handle).

I have a very large composting area, about 6 ft (1.8 m) square, and as green material is cleared off the plot I spread this to make a layer of about 4–5 in (10–12 cm) thick. At this point I go and collect some well-rotted horse manure, which I tip all over the green layer. Then I add further green waste, gradually building up a kind of 'McWalton' sandwich of alternating layers throughout the summer months until I reach the top. This is left to rot all winter, breaking down into a very nice friable mixture for digging in the following spring.

For me, finding a source of manure is a weekend job in summer, when I go scouting to discover where people have the stuff to give away freely. There are still plenty of stables and other places around where you can find it, even though they may not be within the valley. On those mornings I take Anthea along with her yellow Marigold gloves, and her job is to hold the bags open – there's nothing worse than trying to fork manure into a plastic bag on your own because you always end up missing the bag, which makes hard work of the job. I aim to get about twelve bags in two journeys.

No wood, please!

 SOMETHING YOU NEED to watch out for when obtaining stable manure (not 'buying', you notice: no thrifty allot-menteer would actually pay for a waste product) is that the horses haven't been kept on wood shavings or sawdust. These take a long time to break down, seriously depleting the ground of nitrogen as they do so.

I was caught out several years ago when I was given a big supply of stable manure that included wood shavings. For weeks and weeks I went and collected it, and dug it into the ground the following spring. The result was one of my worst seasons: potatoes and beans went yellow because they were struggling for nitrogen, the potato crop was just a lot of tiny little tubers, and I had a very poor onion year too. If you can stack the stuff for several years until it's well rotted, it will eventually do the ground good, but manure based on hay or straw breaks down much faster with no ill effects.

As well as collecting all the green waste off the allotment to go into the main compost heap, we save all our kitchen waste apart from cooked food scraps. Peelings and vegetable offcuts, teabags and fruit cores all end up in a caddy outside my back door with a bag inside it, and when that's full it gets emptied into one of two special upright bins on the allotment. When one is full and rotting down, I switch to the other. The resulting compost goes into the greenhouse beds, which I empty and change every two years.

I always find it strange that, even now with all the emphasis on recycling, there are so few who actually collect waste and manufacture their own compost. You won't find many plots up on the allotments with compost heaps, although there's been a little improvement in recent times since the local council have been offering deals on basic plastic bins.

Because of this lack of interest I tend to inherit a lot of compostable waste from other people. It could be put out for recycling by the council, who will collect from the gate, but I've told everybody they can give it to me for my heap. And that adds to the amount we collect ourselves – although it can be a pain in the summer when everyone mows their lawns and puts black bags containing their grass cuttings at the end of my drive!

There are often other sources of manure, if you look around. Tommy Parr, my early mentor, always kept animals or birds – for many years he was a keen canary exhibitor as well as a big vegetable showman. Later on he bred show rabbits, and after his death his son Ray continued to keep dozens of them in two large sheds in the garden. These needed cleaning out regularly, of course, and every Sunday morning at nine o'clock, give or take thirty seconds, you could guarantee my phone would ring and it would be Ray.

'Are you going to the allotments today, Terry?'

'Ray, I go to the allotments *every* Sunday,' I'd say.

'Well, I've just cleaned the hutches out, and when you come past you'll find there's four bags of rabbit manure here for you.'

So every Sunday morning without fail, for about fifty weeks of the year, I had a generous supply of straw mixed with rabbit pellets, which is a wonderful natural fibrous material to add to everything else on my compost heap as an activator, the concentration of urine and pellets helping all the other stuff to break down.

One of the guys down on the allotments in Trealaw kept pigeons, and whenever he cleaned out the loft he used to ring to say he had three or four bags of pigeon manure for me to collect. That's diabolical stuff, very acid and high in ammonia, and the smell is almost lethal. Within minutes of loading the bags into the boot the car would be stinking, which didn't amuse Anthea one bit if she was with me. But it was a valuable booster on top of the rabbit-straw manure, because it was so vicious and high in nitrogen that the straw would break down very quickly.

Unfortunately change is a fact of life. Ray has passed on and his rabbits are gone. The pigeons went, too, so that was the end of those sources of humus.

That's always been the way here. During the late fifties and early sixties we could depend on manure from the abattoir in nearby Ton Pentre. Any day of the week when they were cleaning out the abattoir a lorry would arrive at the gate, and in return for a drink the driver would cart and tip a lorryload of fresh manure near your plot. This was useful provided you had room to stack it for nearly a year before use. Unfortunately that's gone and there are now no abattoirs anywhere in the vicinity of the allotments.

In the fifties there were large stables for the pit ponies at the colliery in Llwynypia, and the people there were very happy to bring the manure half a mile across to the allotments. But with the demise of the collieries and the coal board, the pit ponies went.

Rhondda farms have never been a reliable source of manure because they tend to be on the mountain tops, too far for the farmer to cart it down to us. Most of them are sheep farms anyway, and sheep aren't usually penned like horses or cows, so you don't get a lavish supply. Very few people used to keep horses, which was an expensive hobby, although some have them now for their children to ride. So at times there has been no nearby source of manure in any quantity, especially during the seventies.

Later several of us on the plots formed a little cooperative, and we'd hire a lorry, find a large source of manure and then spend a whole day collecting it – one loading, one driving, one tipping, one throwing – for a reasonably cheap price. And for a while we got together to buy lorryloads of mushroom compost, but that all came to an end eventually (see Chapter 11).

So I was left wondering what I could do now to improve the soil and keep fertility levels up. Then, a few years ago, I went to a lecture at Pencoed College given by a guy who was growing his vegetables completely organically, and that proved to be another turning point for me. He convinced me that digging the plot and leaving large swathes of ground empty all winter meant much of the goodness leached out, especially in our extremely wet part of the world.

He introduced me to green manure crops, plants sown deliberately to cover the soil and protect it until they are dug in to rot down and form humus. In particular, he reckoned I needed to grow 'fixers', plants that preserve fertility by absorbing the soil nutrients that would otherwise have washed out, and 'lifters', plants that extract nutrients from the subsoil, bringing them up to make them available for later crops after they are dug in.

Various green manure crops are good for these purposes, especially clover and mustard, but mustard needs just the right conditions to grow fairly quickly, while clover works best over a two- or three-year cycle and I can't afford to give up part of my plot for that amount of time. 'Westerwolds' rye was his suggestion, a quick-growing perennial rye grass that produces a large root mass and is ideal for autumn sowing. Now, when I dig out my potatoes in mid- or late August, I just rake those large areas of ground down and sow the rye grass broadcast over the surface. In a reasonable year it will grow to about 4–5 in (10–12 cm) high, although it can get taller after a mild winter and need digging in sooner than normal (otherwise it would take longer to break down). It's a brilliant plant. Its foliage protects the soil surface, the roots absorb nutrients, and when you turn it into the ground during February you've virtually got horse manure without the horse. By the time you fork through again in April ready for planting there's a very friable mixture of roots and green material already rotting down.

I still use animal manure to top up fertility levels because there's never quite enough from green manure alone. But I find one of the big advantages of the rye is that its 'rescued' fertility is available for crops that don't relish animal manure – carrots, parsnips and the other root crops, for example. These occupy about one-third of my plot each year and that's where I concentrate it.

Another third contains the winter vegetables, and the remaining third I winter-dig and dress heavily with loads of horse or cow manure or whatever I can get my hands on. Here I grow onions and peas, and dig the bean trenches. I don't tend to manure cabbage ground because I think that makes the soil slightly more acid, which encourages clubroot: instead my brassicas follow the peas and beans without any extra manure.

Not that I'm a big brassica grower. I don't grow many cabbages: they're difficult to keep safe from the pigeons in winter, and during the summer there's so much else to eat – beans, peas, salads and so on – that cabbage isn't so welcome. But I do grow a few to follow my broad beans, which finish reasonably early in the season. I just cut down their topgrowth and set the cabbage plants between the roots, which have fixed nitrogen from the air and release it again as they rot.

Gradual change

'GROWING YOUR OWN FERTILITY' with green manures is a cunning way to boost crops and also fortify soil conditions in the longer term. Usually when anyone changes back to organic there's a distinct slump in yield because you need to restore the underlying fertility of the soil after using inorganics for a long time.

With all the goodness leached out, it can take a while to build up that fertility again, and inevitably there will be weaker crops at first because the soil is not so productive. Weaker plants are more susceptible to pests, so there can be a double negative effect. This can discourage some people, who may prefer to change gradually over a few years.

Unfortunately some organic enthusiasts can be very

intolerant, unable to see any alternative to immediately using organics exclusively and convinced that people who do otherwise are major polluters and environmental vandals. I think that's a bit extreme. In the long term organic has to be the better way for everyone and everything, because you know exactly what you're putting in and getting out. But I have to admit it's more labour-intensive because you need to keep a close eye on things all the time. And you need patience: when everything in the soil has been destroyed it takes a while to heal and restore the balance.

After I gave up inorganics it took me three or four years to get back to where I had been before. Onions were very disappointing initially, with embarrassingly small bulbs. I had always buried some humus under them to hold the moisture, because they're quite shallow rooted, but their former size and quality came from the effect of the artificials, especially the liberal doses during May and June to help them make maximum leaf growth – every leaf is another layer on the bulb, so the more leaves the better.

Sulphate of ammonia used to produce plenty of large leaves and some really cracking bulbs. But when I suddenly stopped using chemicals, my onions looked more like shallots, and I was struggling to keep them growing throughout the season. What made it worse was that others around me on the allotments were still doing things the inorganic way, and the difference in quality was even more obvious. Not to mention the hurt pride!

I took a lot of stick from the others while converting to this apparently newfangled way of growing things. As they walked by the plot they'd pass classic comments like 'Not growing much this year then, Terry?' or 'You're into these mini-vegetables now, are you?' or even 'There won't be much to keep you going this winter, Terry.' To make it worse, I was only one plot in from the gate, so everyone had to pass my patch on the way to theirs. It didn't do a lot for my reputation as the longest serving member there, always expected to grow very accept-able produce, as I had done in my selling days.

But my father's words spurred me on. 'Terry,' he used to say, 'gardening is all about patience and perseverance.'

So I persisted, and I can truly say that I've now achieved my goal of growing excellent, almost totally organic produce. One day I might even manage to give up using those little blue slug pellets, and finally reach the pinnacle of completely poison-free cultivation.

Organic seeds

THERE'S A STRONG MOVE towards using organically raised seeds, though I'm a bit sceptical. I'm not convinced you can guar-antee seeds *are* organic. You need insects to pollinate the flowers in order to get seeds, and they fly around all over the place, so unless you have a massive great place fenced off from the outside world you can't be sure a bee hasn't gone from one type of plant to another. It's like organic honey: how do you control where the bee goes?

I'm not sure that it matters anyway. I can't see how an organic seed is fundamentally any different from a normal seed, because the genetic material is the same and that's all a seed brings with it. It seems far more important to avoid 'genetically modified' seeds, because there the character of the future plant has been tampered with, which again opens up the uncertainties of long-term consequences.

Exactly the problem we had with inorganic gardening, in fact. Do we ever learn?

There's a greater acceptance of organics on the plots these days, and a lot of people don't reckon to use insecticides at all. That's the first and probably the most important thing to change, but there are still a lot of users of Growmore, although sulphate of ammonia has dropped off considerably, mainly because people now tend to realize it's a quick fix and not a real food.

This change of heart is being reflected nationally, with more organic produce being sold in shops and garden centres. Regular farmers' markets are held throughout the country, offering opportunities to buy and sell home-grown, organic produce. And the demand for allotments is still on the increase, with most sites now reporting waiting lists, particularly of people wanting to grow their stuff organically because of the unavailability or high price of organic vegetables in shops. It's an enormously encouraging trend.

I find these days people look at my plot, see that I'm getting pretty good results now and ask what I'm doing, and when they see that organics do actually work they're sufficiently convinced to try that method themselves. My yields are back up to where they were, and I'm actually picking more runner beans because there are fewer flowers falling off without setting seed.

I have to admit some plants looked more luscious when they were grown with chemicals: a cabbage, for example, was always a deeper green than it is now. But it's still a green vegetable and good enough for my needs, especially as I know what has gone into it. And that's what's important.

Terry's Tip for August

Rhubarb soup

No, THIS ISN'T ONE of Anthea's recipes! I've discovered a brew of rhubarb leaves that I use to water cabbages and other brassicas, both to keep the cabbage white butterfly away and as a bonus to provide some kind of feed – I'm not sure exactly what it supplies, though: I just know that Brussels sprouts watered with this soup have done better for me than ever before, so I'm keeping an open mind about it.

I have an old black plastic dustbin which I three-quarters fill with water. As I harvest rhubarb stems I trim off the leaves and add them to the water, giving them a good stir before replacing the lid. I keep adding more, stirring twice weekly, until after a few weeks the soup begins to smell slightly evil: a sure sign that it's ready.

Use it neat in a watering can fitted with a rose, and water all over the tops of your brassica plants, including swedes and anything else likely to host cabbage root fly or the white butterflies. When the dustbin is only about a quarter full, top it back up with water, and keep adding more leaves and stirring the mixture to rejuvenate it.

This brew seems to deter the butterfly from laying its eggs, and the run-off down to the roots discourages the root fly from laying. It doesn't stop white fly as this tends to collect on the undersides of leaves, nor will it control mealy bug, which forms in some less accessible places on the leaves. But no single method controls everything. Reapply frequently – especially after wet weather, which dilutes the unique fragrance of the soup and hence its efficacy.

Anthea's Recipe for August

Cucumber and Tomato Relish

(900w microwave recipe)

GREENHOUSE CROPS ARE usually coming thick and fast by now, so you should be able to supply the cucumber, tomatoes and green pepper from under glass, together with one of this year's onions that needs harvesting early because of its thick or split neck.

- 1 cucumber
- 1 level tsp salt
- ¾ pint (450 ml) cider vinegar

- **8 oz (225 g) granulated sugar**
- **½ tsp curry powder**
- **¼ tsp cayenne pepper**
- **¼ tsp ground ginger**
- **1 level tbsp chopped mint**
- **4 oz (125 g) sultanas**
- **1 lb (450 g) ripe tomatoes**
- **1 small green pepper**
- **1 medium onion**

Wash, peel and chop the cucumber into small pieces. Place in a basin and sprinkle with the salt to remove some of the moisture. Put to one side.

Put the vinegar in a large microwavable dish and cook on high until boiling. Add the sugar, stir until dissolved, and add the spices.

Drain the cucumber, finely chop the onion, de-seed the pepper and dice, skin the tomatoes and chop into small pieces.

Add all ingredients to the vinegar, sugar and spice mixture, stir well, and cook on high for 20–30 mins (the shorter the time, the crunchier the relish).

Put into sterilized jars, and seal when cold.

CHAPTER NINE

The Penultimate Plot

I WENT ORGANIC in the early 1980s, after my father had died and while I was looking after his two plots. I think he would have approved of my giving up artificial fertilizers and chemical insecticides: all I was doing really was returning to the style of gardening he used in the first place, back in the late forties after he came to the valley from the Midlands and afterwards while I was learning by his side.

It was time to settle down but something was niggling at me. I had a good job, a wife and a growing family, and my father's two good plots to tend and crop to the best of my ability to keep us well fed. Perhaps I missed all the excitement and stimulus of running my earlier vegetable empire, or maybe it was simply that stage in life when things run so smoothly the days begin to seem humdrum, but for a while I had the urge to change direction and go in for gardening full-time.

I enjoyed the challenge of growing things, and I'd toyed on and off with the idea of doing something more with the allotments. Then a garden centre on the old Cardiff Road came up for sale, a rough and ready sort of place that was becoming rather run down.

It was very tempting. In those days there weren't many garden centres or big supermarkets selling the selection of plants they do now, and this was the only place in our district. It didn't stock a vast range of goods – no big concrete ornaments or pools or garden furniture – nor did the guy have a posh café, which people now seem to expect.

But you could usually find what you wanted there. He had several big greenhouses where he grew everything and sold bedding plants in the spring, a large outdoor area full of shrubs and larger plants, and a shop selling fresh vegetables. As you drove in you passed his big fields where he grew cauliflowers and potatoes and other produce.

This seriously appealed to my market gardening instincts, and the way I saw it I could sell plants throughout the summer, like a nursery, while growing vegetables to sell in the garden centre shop. That was the plan I was mulling over, and at one point I was perhaps 60 per cent certain I could make a go of it.

Common sense and caution prevailed, though. When I looked hard at the idea in terms of business viability, it was obvious I'd only have six or seven months of the year in which to earn sufficient income to carry me over the rest. One bad spring or a wet season and I could be back to square one; two poor years and I'd be in real trouble.

Although gardening had been my first love in life, I reasoned that my job in industry was fulfilling, I had a steady income, a good company and boss to work for, and I actually enjoyed the job. I could carry on looking after the allotment in my spare time without any risk, simply growing for home use and to enjoy myself.

And I was glad in the end I didn't take a gamble, because later they put in a motorway which bypassed the place and took away all the passing trade. Garden centres began to spring up everywhere, big places selling stuff at prices I can't even buy it for to sell on the allotments. Everything in the business became very competitive, with places fighting to get customers through the door. And gardeners are the tightest people under the sun, willing to drive around and use a gallon of petrol to save a few pence several miles away.

So I carried on as before, earning my living in industry by day and spending most of my leisure time on my father's two allotments. At first my brother Eric came and gave me a hand there: he called in regularly to see our mother and came up to the plots for a whiff of air and some outdoor exercise, but after she died there was no real home to revisit, and he became less and less interested in the allotments.

The age difference between Eric and me is ten years and a week, so throughout our lives we've tended to pass each other 'like ships in the night': when I was only eight he went to university, and then qualified as a physics teacher and disappeared to his first teaching job in Wimbledon while I was still in my early teens. We had only fleeting contact while we were young.

Eric returned to teach in the Rhondda, but soon got married and set up house close by in Tonypandy, and apart from odd meetings at our parents' house and some brief get-togethers on the allotments, we mostly led separate lives. It's a sad but familiar fact that work pressures and diverging interests keep siblings apart during early life, and only reunions back home with parents on special occasions recreate any sense of family. Once parents have gone and that focus disappears, links can be more difficult to maintain.

But since we both retired we have met more frequently: there's our common enthusiasm for bowls, and Eric comes up to my plot most Saturday mornings now and takes an interest in what's going on there. The Walton link with gardening must still be part of his make-up, his return to the allotments a kind of homecoming!

Like Eric, I felt that the old family connections had suddenly vanished after our mam died.

And then Joe Vickery decided he was giving up his plot. He had been there for years and was a superb gardener, one of the neatest guys you've ever seen in your life. His plot was pristine, he'd built a greenhouse for himself, and everything was in really good shape. But his son-in-law had built a new house close to where Joe lived, with acres of ground where he'd be able to carry on gardening, so his allotment became available. Some of the members said to me, 'Well, why don't you go nearer the gate? You're the longest-serving member here, why not move?'

I pointed out that I had sentimental attachments to my father's old plots, which were very good and down on the lowest row, about halfway to the gate. But they argued Joe had a nice greenhouse there, the plot was immaculate and had been well tended for years, so it was in a good fertile state, and it was only one in from the gate. After a lot of thought I began to see that it made sense. I wouldn't be letting anybody down. So finally I made up my mind to move there.

The prospect of leaving those two plots tugged at my heart-strings. They had been my father's for so many years and held countless memories for me, especially that corner where I had started my allotment career all that time ago. As I continued working them after my father had gone, there had been many moments when I'd stop and wonder if this was how Dad used to do a particular job.

On days when I feel like reminiscing, I still stroll over to the old homestead and recall past times with much fondness. But life moves on, and change is good for us. Memories can never be erased, though.

Part of the attraction of the new plot was undoubtedly the superb greenhouse Joe had built. I'd put up one of my own, and I didn't want to move to a plot without one and be forced to start all over again. Joe's had been made out of old window frames so it had opening lights everywhere to provide plenty of ventilation in the summer months to help keep mildew at bay. (I leave them an inch or two ajar most of the time and get very little trouble.)

The greenhouse also had a concrete path in the middle, down between the beds. In summer, when I water I always pour two or three canfuls up the path as well as using my power spray to spread a fine mist over the plants and keep the air moist. Using plenty of water ensures that red spider mite, which thrives in dry conditions, is never a problem there.

Joe's greenhouse was also more spacious. This meant that removing the side shoots of tomatoes became much easier. All tomatoes throw lots of side shoots, until a plant can become quite unmanageable, so it's usual to remove these while they are still small. They tend to form at the base of leaves, especially just beyond a flower truss, and are easily overlooked if you don't check the plant from top to bottom. Pinch them out from cordon (single-stem) plants to keep the main stem going straight up, without competition. There's no need to do this with cherry-fruited kinds and bush ('determinate') varieties, except to keep the plant under control: the bushier these plants, the greater their yield.

I couldn't resist this appealing greenhouse upgrade, and it was that which finally persuaded me to move. All I had to do then to be fully equipped was add a shed alongside – the one I was leaving behind wasn't suitable for the space on the new plot, so I joined the crowd of allotment builders and knocked up somewhere to keep my tools.

Water management

NEXT TO MY BUILDINGS I arranged a row of water barrels, linked to each other with overflows and aligned to collect all the rainwater running off the roofs. In a dry summer I put the hosepipe in the first one and let them all fill. As this water coming from the mountain is icy cold, I leave it in the barrels until the following evening to warm up and then water my plants with a watering can.

I don't tend to water every day, except in the greenhouse. Outdoors I give things a good soaking every two or three days if it's been particularly dry, and I only concentrate on certain crops. I never water root vegetables like parsnips and carrots because I don't want them forking; I prefer to force them to grow straight down in search of water. But beans and onions in particular need a copious and regular supply if they are to grow well, and it's important to keep seedlings, recent transplants and leafy crops like salads well watered too.

So I took over Joe's plot when he left, and eventually I gave up one of my father's plots and then the other shortly afterwards, to concentrate on the plot I've now been on for about sixteen years. Its completely different shape caused me all sorts of complications at first when planting: in the first year I grew too much of things like early broad beans, and as spring progressed I quickly ran out of space for later crops. But after three seasons there, memories of the planting regime on the old plots were dimmer and I was back in control, settling in happily.

There have been several opportunities since for me to move along just one more plot and get to the gate, but there was no real point. That plot didn't have a greenhouse, and in any case the old incentive to move along with seniority has completely gone. There's no reason any more.

Up to the 1950s there were never any buildings on a plot, no greenhouses or sheds, and you simply cultivated the ground. Under the old strict rules the plot you moved to was always identical to the one you left, and the only reason for moving was to get closer to plot no. 1, nearer the gate and more accessible from the road.

But times have changed, the rules have been relaxed to encourage new tenants, and these people tend to be builders who put up such elaborate greenhouses and sheds that when somewhere else becomes available they're reluctant to give up what they've built. Whenever a plot's empty we put a notice up inviting applications, but the good gardeners don't tend to move now because they've got their plot just as they want it, equipped with various buildings. Although the old rule of seniority still applies when there are multiple applications, newer members tend to come in anywhere on the site now.

The old committee members would probably have a fit if

they could come back now, and would think us very lax in the way we run the site. Certainly things have changed dramatically from the earlier, more rigid days.

I took over as secretary in 1977, and Derek Lavis, who was an excellent gardener and a firm committee member who always spoke his mind, became chairman about the same time. He and I worked well together and our partnership continued into the nineties. Even though there was a full committee, it rarely met, and Derek and I would run all the affairs between us. When he gave up his plot in the mid-nineties I was somehow left to make the decisions on my own. I call a committee meeting whenever there's any dispute, although the other members always say, 'But what would you do then?'

There isn't a lot of committee business these days, anyway. At a recent AGM we did decide to do something about three plots that were not in a very good state. I called everyone together and we went to inspect the plots (just like in the old days), and decided we'd send their tenants a letter to say that if the plots weren't cultivated they'd be allocated to people on the waiting list. One member responded by tidying his plot, one left and the third fought the eviction through the local council: he was given a further month to clean up the plot but failed to meet that deadline and was duly evicted, his plot going to a new tenant.

Length of membership is no longer the sole criterion when allocating a plot. Our once inflexible rule of progression by seniority was changed some years ago when we had plots lying idle. New members would often come in, scratch about half-heartedly for a bit and wait for a clean plot to become available so they could put in to move on the grounds that they'd been there for a couple of years and were senior. So we changed the rules to allow gardeners to move on the basis of merit.

For many years anyone who walked in looking for a plot was almost certain to leave armed with a key to the gate and a tenancy agreement in hand. But now there's a waiting list – which at one point went up to five, although it's now back to three – getting a plot means waiting until someone gives up, and that can be quite unpredictable. With willing tenants waiting in the wings, it helps to have eviction as a penalty for failure to look after a plot.

That's just one instance of the radical change in management style forced on us by circumstances. The old committee members, who were looked upon as father figures and ran the place with a rod of iron, all left about the time the allotments began to decline. Tommy Parr and my father were the last bastions of the old way, and after they went in the mid-seventies it became more and more difficult to apply the rules rigidly.

New members had a different outlook, and there were some applying for tenancies who couldn't or wouldn't do a whole plot. There was no point turning them down while we had nobody else waiting to join us: better to have half or a third of a plot cultivated than total dereliction.

That was my philosophy throughout the eighties until demand began to revive, because I felt we had to temper the rules with common sense to keep people gardening. We even contemplated letting what we were going to call 'community plots', where an allotment would be split into three for people who wanted smaller amounts to do. But suddenly there was an upturn in interest and we didn't need to do that to get the ground occupied.

There's still a shop on site, and our storekeeper, Albie, lives nearby, where he can keep an eye on things. We now deal only in bulk materials, though, because the garden centres and supermarkets all sell gardening supplies extremely cheaply, often as loss leaders. And we run a seed-ordering system: in September I have a batch of catalogues sent and distributed to the members, they give me their orders and we get a discount depending on quantity.

All twenty-five available plots are under cultivation, and after ninety years of continuous occupation most of the plots are in reasonably good shape, with a good depth of fertile topsoil over the pure clay beneath. I rarely have to use my foot these days when I'm digging (just as well, since I'm not inclined by nature to 'put the boot in'!).

In fact, most people who come in don't have to struggle like they used to, which has to be a good thing. Anyone taking over during the doldrums of the seventies faced a jungle, which could be very demoralizing: they'd get something planted and then come back in a week or two, only to find the weeds had smothered their small seeds. Their heart would go out of the job then and they would often give up.

Something I found strange when moving plots was how their differences in shape could affect the way things were grown. I could have rows right across my father's long, narrow plots, whereas the one I have now is extremely wide, almost as wide as it's long, and a full row across is in excess of 30 ft (9 m). I consider weeding to be one of the more daunting chores in gardening, and the longer the row the worse the job can be. With short rows you soon get to the end and feel elated, ready to tackle the next, but if you're two-thirds of the way down a long row and the weeds ahead are still thick, you really think you're never going to reach the end.

So on my new, wider plot I moved the beanpoles from their usual place at the bottom and re-erected them across the middle to split the plot approximately in half. Now I have two smaller 'plots' and can grow everything *down* the mountainside in shorter rows, about 12 ft (3.5 m) long. It's all psychological, of course, and just a way to make the job manageable!

Short manageable rows are more sensible when you're growing for your own use, making space for a greater variety of crops and more successional harvests. It was different when I was growing only a few crops for regular sale, when I could quickly clear a full 30 ft (9 m) row of some things. Shorter rows are also easier to mulch, a technique that has become very popular generally for keeping the soil moist and protected from hot sun and heavy rain.

We have never tended to use mulches on the allotments, simply because we don't have the large quantities of suitable material to spare. All the bracken and manure we collected was dug into the bean trenches as a bulky soil improver, and there wasn't enough left over.

Annual digging was part of everyone's routine, just single digging in most cases although many gardeners used to trench for certain crops. Now, digging can be the most monotonous job on the allotment, particularly the big winter dig. You set a steady rhythm of push, turn, breathe, and this goes on continuously until you seem to drift into a hypnotic trance. This is the time to let yourself daydream, thinking of those things that give you the most pleasure (no, I'm not letting you into *my* secret thoughts!).

But beware if, like me, you have a robin as your winter companion. He swoops down on every spadeful, seizing any unearthed grub or worm. One careless slip of the spade, and he's a robin no more.

The alternative practice of 'no dig' gardening has a huge following, but not here: it's quite unsuitable for our clay-based allotments, where it's essential for the well-being of the soil that we turn the ground over and leave it in large lumps, exposed to all the winter frosts and rain, which break it down into a friable material. This is then easily forked over in the spring to provide a fine tilth and comfortable bed for all those vulnerable seeds to begin their lives.

I still trench the ground annually for runner beans, sweet peas and chrysanthemums, to get manure deep down at the base of their roots. I dig out the trench in the autumn, fill it with compostable materials and manure, and then leave it open for two or three weeks to settle and compact a little before backfilling it with the excavated soil. The result looks rather like a burial mound at first, but gradually sinks until the ground is level again and ready for planting.

The runner bean routine

 MY RUNNER BEANS GET special treatment. I don't rotate them round the plot like other crops, because I grow them on a well-anchored permanent framework of scaffolding poles. Into their trench I lose all the waste material from clearing my back and front gardens at home and from my son's garden, together with the contents of old hanging baskets, all topped off with a thick layer of well-rotted manure so that there's a good 15 in (38 cm) or more of waste material under the surface.

I leave that to settle for a couple of weeks before backfilling it. Since the beans have been grown in the same place, trenched every winter, for sixteen years, it must be a particularly fertile spot now. I don't know if the bed continues to get better each year; I think it probably peaked quite a long time ago. However, the plants provide plenty to eat all summer and to freeze, with a surplus to give away.

For years I grew one complete row of runners and half a row of French beans, but these days I grow half a row each of French and runner beans, and use the other poles for sweet peas.

My onions stay in the same place for about four or five years before I move them to their other bed – I only grow them in two areas. I build up the ground for them until it's extremely rich, and then start to do the same in the other area, moving them as a precaution against getting root rot on the plants. I haven't had it yet and to make sure I don't get it I feel it's a sound policy to keep moving them every so often. It's the same with strawberries, which are best moved every three years to avoid building up disease.

Everything else I rotate annually around the plot and always have done, and I keep a plan up on the wall of the shed to remind me where everything should go. This is particularly important with potatoes, which are planted in well-manured ground, and then root crops can follow the next year without getting disorders from having their toes in recent manure.

Potatoes and blight

I KEEP SEPARATE PATCHES for the various kinds of potatoes because they need different treatment. First earlies come fast and seldom develop problems because they're too early for the potato blight, whereas second earlies are sometimes borderline, and with maincrops, which take much longer to mature, blight can be a real nuisance.

August is the critical month, when blight can spread like wildfire from plot to plot on allotments, and you often have a hell of a job keeping maincrop potatoes totally clean. The problem is that there is no organic fungicide for treating the disease if you're chemical-free. I used to use copper sulphate many years ago, and you can buy other chemical remedies now, but I prefer to control it by cutting off blighted leaves and disposing of them with the waste put out for the refuse collector, and then harvesting the crop earlier than usual.

For that reason I tend not to grow so many main-crops these days. First earlies such as 'Arran Pilot' keep us going as I dig them steadily from June onwards, while later kinds like 'Charlotte' and 'Kestrel' – a tremendous cropper, as good as any maincrop – will usually take us on well into the winter. The potato foliage or 'haulm' goes on my compost heap if it's clean, but I'd rather be cautious with the haulm from maincrops so I burn that instead.

Fewer potatoes are grown on the plots these days as eating habits have changed, but not the pleasure of harvesting them. Digging for potatoes is like unearthing buried treasure, and you never know what you're going to find once you start. But no matter how thorough you are, you can't get them all out in one go. You may think you've cleared them, and then you put the fork back in, shake the soil about and find four or five more, often bigger ones that were missed first time round.

And Murphy's Law ('if anything can go wrong, it will') definitely applies to digging potatoes, because you invariably stick one of the prongs on the fork through the best tuber. Some varieties have a spreading habit, so you dig further away, and others are more compact with all their tubers clustered together, but it makes little difference: I'll put the fork in and hit the best potato nine times out of ten.

And the tiny ones that always slip through are the worst gardener's weed, coming up the following year somewhere awkward, like the middle of a row of carrots, so that when you try to get out this tiny tuber, no bigger than a marble, you cause a great eruption of disturbed soil because the root is so big.

Even so, there are many other crops I'd give up before potatoes. There's always room for a row of first earlies in the smallest of plots. They'll be out of the way in June and then you can use that ground again, which I try to do wherever I can. I'm a greedy gardener and usually aim to get double crops off at least half my plot. Most of the early potatoes will leave you time to sow or plant another crop afterwards, broad beans likewise, and I tend not to plan large special areas for salads because they can go in as follow-on crops wherever ground becomes available.

That's how I came unstuck when I entered the allotment

competition for the first time in 2005. I was persuaded to have a go by the television crew filming *The Big Dig* for BBC2, who thought an element of competition would enhance the programme. Our local Rhondda Cynon Taff Council holds an annual contest to find the best allotments in each area and then select an overall winner. Roger, who has one of the best plots on our site, and I both entered, with the programme following our efforts to win and the judging of the plots. Neither of us is naturally competitive, but it all made good television.

One of the things the judges check is the rotation system, or lack of it, on the plot, and when they came to mine in July they said, 'But you're not following the rules!'

And I said, 'Well, the reason I'm bending the strict rules of rotation is because these are my second crops. I planned what I wanted to grow early – potatoes, beans, roots and so on – and they were all rotated in the usual way. But when they're finished I don't leave that area fallow. By July some of my second early potatoes are out, and that ground has now gone down to salad crops. My broad beans have gone, and where they were is now cabbages, which were not part of the overall plan: I've got a main brassica bed limed ready, but this is an overflow planted to follow another crop. So I can't rotate strictly according to the book because I'm getting two crops in a season, for example beans and cabbages from the same bed.'

To me it makes sense, while the soil after lifting potatoes is nice and friable with plenty of fertility left in there, to plant some salad crops – some small beet and some lettuce or radish – because they'll revel in the perfect tilth and leftover good-ness. But according to the judges you should reserve an area specially for salad crops. They were looking for orthodox groupings of crops, which I don't have.

They were happy with the quality of the crops, and marked

me high on the layout and cleanliness of the plot, the standard of composting and environmental matters. But because I don't toe the line on rotation I came fourth. Roger, who is a very neat and meticulous gardener but has never shown a competitive streak, was very put out by the judges' comments about his plot. After a heated discussion with them he stormed off, vowing never to enter a competition again.

By making the ground crop for as long as possible each season (in this part of the world only four to four and a half months at its peak) I try to maximize the produce for eating, storing and preserving, to keep us all year round. I never quite make it and there's usually a gap about May, when the winter and stored crops are finished and we're waiting for the first of the new season's harvest. But you can still get a hell of a lot off a typical allotment.

One way to do this is by double-cropping; another is to protect with cloches early and late to extend the season. I've tried forcing strawberries on the plot, but that isn't really worthwhile, although I do cloche a row or two when they start to make some decent growth, just to bring them on a week or two earlier (but you have to be careful because once they flower you need to allow pollinating insects in).

Cloches are a great help, especially those made of fleece because this lets water through (polythene dries out everything underneath too quickly). I cover most things with fleece laid over hoops, and when crops don't need it any more in early June, I cut the sheet in half lengthways and stake it right round my carrots like a corral to keep the carrot root fly off.

I try to stretch the lettuce season by covering the plants with fleece, starting with the first January sowings of butter-head types, sown in my greenhouse and set out in April under a cloche for cutting about mid-May. Then in April I sow my first lollo rosso and my first icebergs in the greenhouse to plant in the second week in May, after which I sow more every couple of weeks. With a bit of help from Mother Nature and a lot of luck I can cut lettuce from the beginning of May until the end of September.

It helps when raising seedlings for the allotment if you have an understanding partner (thank you, Anthea!) who is prepared to let you use part of the airing cupboard for germinating the more expensive or fussy stuff. I start my tomatoes, cucumbers, courgettes and other large-seeded tender things in there, and after a couple of days in that warmth they're through.

Like most plotholders I don't have a heated greenhouse at the allotments because it's not so easy to keep an eye on things there or pop up in the evening after you're heard a bad weather forecast. The greenhouse on the allotment tends to be my cold house, and when the seedlings are ready they leave my heated greenhouse at home and move up there.

True love

USING THE AIRING CUPBOARD for propagation came about by accident several years ago. I'd been having problems getting my tomato seed to germinate because I couldn't keep the temperature constant in the greenhouse. The instructions on the seed packet got me thinking that our airing cupboard had the precise amount of warmth I needed to start the seeds off, so I asked Anthea, 'Would you mind if I move some of your towels to one side to put in a tray of tomato seed?'

I survived the few expletives that followed, and was granted a little of this heated space. And it worked beautifully, so much so that little by little over the years an increasing number of seed trays have been finding a home in there during early spring. I understand that Anthea's now contemplating having a new airing cupboard built for herself and leaving this one to me.

The situation's made worse by the fact that germinating seeds must be taken out promptly into the light as they appear, or the dark warm conditions will draw the seedlings and make them too tall and lanky. Moving them straight to the greenhouse is too drastic, so they all end up on the landing windowsill, and I try to convince Anthea they look more appealing than the artificial flowers that normally stand there.

I think she's quite relieved when all my tender seeds are sown and growing normally, so she can take full possession of her airing cupboard and reclaim her windowsill.

Another way to make the most of your crops is to eat only what is in season. I don't like all these things that are flown halfway round the world, notching up thousands of air miles and totally lacking in flavour. Eating an imported strawberry in February is not my idea of pleasure, and I'd rather wait for a ripe sun-warmed dishful off my own plants at the right time.

We do eat beans almost all year round because I grow enough to freeze and they're extremely good from the freezer, especially French beans. But otherwise we have whatever is in season, which in the winter months means swedes, leeks, parsnips, Brussels sprouts, the remnants of the carrot crop until around Christmas, and potatoes, onions or shallots out of store. Winter seems the wrong time of year to eat many salads, and in any case tomatoes are somewhat tasteless then.

Something I've always done every year since I started gardening is provide all the vegetables on the Christmas dinner plate. We used to dig the first early potatoes, par-cook them and roll them in butter, and then keep them in an ice-cream tub in the freezer to roast on Christmas Day. Saving the first potatoes from the start of the season for Christmas seemed almost ritualistic and a real celebration. We don't do that now, though, because I grow maincrops and there are usually plenty of them tucked away in store.

Even though the children aren't always with us these days, we still make something of the Christmas veg each year. My dad would do that, going up on Christmas morning to gather everything, and when we lived a hundred yards away I did the same. But now we're five miles from the plot and the chances are that we'll be having dinner with the family, I harvest on Christmas Eve. A concession to the times perhaps, but when we eat it the veg is still barely twenty-four hours away from growing.

The Walton Christmas lunch is truly special: as well as gathering all the vegetables, I actually prepare them, something that rarely happens at any other time of the year. This is by way of a thank you to Anthea for her patience and understanding throughout the year.

I watch all the family tucking into the vegetables and enjoying them, and a great feeling of satisfaction comes over me when I think that all this sumptuous food has been nurtured on this Rhondda hillside, absorbing vitality from the sun, rain and other elements. Grown exactly as nature intended, it's now releasing all this goodness for the pleasure of my family on this particularly joyous occasion. The empty plates afterwards bear witness to the quality of the home-grown food and crown the sense of gratification. Long may this extra-special celebration continue.

When I was growing to sell I avoided winter vegetables for a number of reasons, one being that they complicated life, occupying the ground for so long and often overlapping with one or more seasonal growing periods. Even now I find they can muddle the rotation and mess up the neat divisions on the plot.

I try sometimes to get them as close together as I can so they're all in one block, leaving the rest clear for me to dig or sow a green manure. But it can be difficult because my leeks tend to go in at one end of the onion bed to keep all the family together, my Brussels and swedes go in the brassica bed, and my parsnips go next to the carrots. This satisfies the rotation groupings from the point of view of preparing the soil and confining certain pests to distinct areas, but it makes the plot look disorganized in late autumn when each rotation section still has bits and pieces lingering on, sometimes into the following spring.

I tried growing winter cabbages for a few years but they were not very successful, simply because of pigeons. You can put nets over them but the mountainside is very exposed, the gales come along and blow them off and the pigeons find the cabbages in no time. I grow Brussels sprouts, but I don't mind if the pigeons feed on their crowns in November because I don't use those, and as long as the sprouts themselves stay clean and are not pecked, that's not a problem.

It was not unusual for the people living in the house adjacent to the allotments to come over for a few plants to grow in their back garden. One day when I was busy weeding on the plot, I looked up and found Jack standing there.

'Do you have any plants left over of those little cabbages that grow on trees?' he asked.

'Which do you mean, Jack?' I replied, bemused.

'You know,' he said, 'they grow up the stem and then you pick them off when they're ready.'

'You mean Brussels sprouts?'

'Aye, that's right.'

'No, I haven't at the moment,' I said. 'It's too early: come back in three weeks.'

He came back in three weeks and had his little cabbages that grow on trees.

The Brussels usually keep going until about February; leeks and swedes last all winter, as do parsnips some years, although in a bad season I may get an outbreak of canker that spoils the roots. April through to June can be a problem, though, if you're aiming for self-sufficiency. It's not worth growing purple sprouting, kale or spring cabbage here in the Rhondda because they are a real magnet for pigeons, and there can be very little during those months unless the swedes, parsnips and leeks last well. I can have cabbage by late May if I grow 'Primo' under a cloche, started in January in the heated greenhouse, and the broad beans come in then as well, or in early June. So May's the really difficult month when we have to eat out of the freezer.

It seems a far cry from my original empire, when activity was concentrated into a hectic summer season and everything was cleared in September (we could depend on my father to feed us through the winter). Now my allotment year lasts a full twelve months, so I've matured into a full-time gardener instead of just a seasonal worker.

That suits me. The plot is a good place to be, even in a winter gale or typical Welsh downpour: there's always someone to talk to and somewhere to shelter, now all the sheds and greenhouses have turned the place into a kind of shanty town. When the weather's nice, there's no finer place to be. As the allotments are sited on the side of the valley, the sun comes on the corner very early in the morning, shines on us all day as it moves round and still favours us while it's setting.

And the view is tremendous, whether you look down across Llwynypia to the hills on the other side of the broad Rhondda valley, or up the valley itself, where you can see the long ribbons of houses hugging the road as it climbs up through Treorchy and Treherbert to the high mountain beyond, all purple and gold in the setting sun.

Gone now are the blackened hillsides scarred with coal waste and debris from the pits: the land reclamation and land-scaping of the nineties has restored the valley to its former splendour. The contours of the land have been altered for ever, but to the casual visitor this brings new beauty to the hillsides. I have viewed all these steady changes from my plot and constantly marvel at the returning scene, the hillsides green once more and trees flourishing again, studding the hills with blossom. A gloomy industrial wasteland has been transformed into a place of breathtaking light and variety, and one of my most precious and enduring memories is witnessing from my hillside allotment the rebirth of the Rhondda over the half century I've been working there.

I'm never going to get to the last plot by the gate now, and I'm not sure that matters any more. Especially as I'm right opposite Albie's allotment café . . .

Terry's Tip for September

Secrets of the leek

WE MAY HAVE BEEN a little late discovering leeks on our valley plots, but we've quickly learned how to grow them to perfection. Here are the key points:

Sow them in a small pan, prick them out into a standard seed tray (thirty-five per tray), and then *pull* them up at planting time to expose their roots. Trim off the growing tips to minimize the shock of transplanting and shorten the bare roots by half to get the plants deeper in their holes.

I make the hole so that about an inch (2.5 cm) of the green remains above the soil, and use a crowbar, not because the ground is hard but you can twist it round to make the sides of the holes firm. Drop a leek in each, make sure the roots touch the bottom of the hole, and then fill the holes with water, leaving them open to gradually fill in.

When the plants are about a foot (30 cm) high, extend their blanch by covering each one with a 6 in (15 cm) length of 3-in- (8-cm-) diameter ducting pipe – a friendly BT engineer should have offcuts you can scrounge. Bury the bottom inch (2.5 cm) in the soil for stability. With 3–4 in (8–10 cm) below ground, plus the extra inside the pipe, your full-grown leeks should end up with good 8–9 in (20–23 cm) pure white shanks.

Anthea's Recipe for September

Marrow Rum

- **I ripe marrow**
- **5–7 lb (2–3 kg) demerara sugar**
- **wine yeast (general purpose)**
- **yeast nutrient**

Choose a really ripe marrow, wipe it clean with a damp cloth, and remove a piece of the stalk end, deep enough for you to scoop out all the seeds and pith to leave a clear cavity.

Fill this with sugar (the amount will depend on the size of marrow), packing it down firmly. Replace the cut endpiece and seal in place with sticky tape.

Suspend the marrow, sealed end uppermost, securely over a jar or jug, and leave for 2–3 weeks.

After this time unseal the end and add more sugar to replace that absorbed into the flesh. Reseal and suspend for 6–7 weeks or until the liquid contents have all dripped into the jug, leaving an empty shell.

Stir the yeast and yeast nutrient into the liquor and then strain into a fermentation jar. Fit an airlock on top and leave until fermentation ceases.

Siphon or strain into a clean fermentation jar, fit a clean airlock and keep for at least a year, by which time it will be very strong and taste like rum.

CHAPTER TEN

Social Life on the Plot

WHEN I WAS WORKING full-time and going straight up to the allotment afterwards, it was not just to unwind and relax but also to keep up with all the routine gardening chores. I must have been a pretty unsociable guy then, because I almost resented anyone coming over and talking to me. I was there to sow the carrots, do a bit of hoeing, pull a few weeds or get a few plants in; I needed to do something useful with my limited time – it might rain the next day and then I wouldn't be able to get on. After hours of talking and answering the phone at work, the last thing I wanted was to chat to somebody else for three-quarters of an hour instead of tending my plot.

Retiring was like a big wake-up call. Suddenly there was no pressure any more, and I had time to be sociable.

The typical pattern these days is that the first thing I do when I get up to the plot is sit down. Albie will have coffee on the go, and we'll chat for maybe twenty minutes before I wander off and do a bit of work. An hour and a half later it'll be 'Kettle's just boiled!' again, and it doesn't matter now that there's all the time in the day. Jobs that used to take me an hour or so might take me four, and that's *not* because of my age.

In fact there's a lot more than gardening taking place on the plots these days. When my father was up there people came along, they worked, they might discuss what they were doing and exchange tips or comment on the weather, but that was all. Since there were very few buildings on the site, there were no obvious meeting places. But over the years the greenhouses and sheds have developed into a small community, and many have become more than just somewhere to grow tomatoes or store materials.

My father was one of the first to build. Even when I was small he had a long, low greenhouse made out of old sash window frames along the top of one of his plots, and that was where he grew his chrysanths. It was roofed with plastic corrugated sheeting, which was relatively cheap in the early days.

And then in 1971, about the time my first son was born, he bought his first Halls greenhouse, a big wooden structure that looked posh and upstanding in those days. I didn't have a greenhouse then – nothing so exotic. There wasn't the time to look after something like that, and I tried to keep my allotment work easy and streamlined.

But then other people began to erect greenhouses and sheds on their plots, home-made buildings that avoided the need to spend much money. Joe Vickery, who had my current plot before me, was a local carpenter and he managed to acquire a large number of ammunition boxes. They were made of wooden panels, ideal for building, and were being sold off for pennies. All you did was buy a quantity of them and knock them apart, and you had the perfect boarding to make a shed for a few pounds.

Fortunately the local council never laid down any stipulations about the size or materials of greenhouses or sheds, possibly because nobody had bothered with them before. But now the idea was catching on, especially as many people in the Rhondda were starting to exchange their sash windows for double glazing, so suddenly there were lots of cast-off building materials going begging.

Back in the fifties and early sixties people never changed a thing, and removing a whole window was a very ambitious undertaking. As people became more affluent, however, they gradually began to look more critically at their homes and entertain the idea of a better-looking front door or windows with double glazing to conserve the heat. Out went the old sashes, which were just the thing for making a shed or greenhouse: all you had to do was knock up a frame to fit these windows in, and then the old front door of a house would become the door of a shed or greenhouse, sometimes complete with a stained glass panel.

There's a standing joke in the valleys that when anybody orders a skip to do some building work, it's delivered *and* taken away empty. No sooner do windows or doors or useful bits of wood come out of the house than they're up on the allotments. We are the skip-raiders of the valleys, always on the alert for anything useful. It's the old spirit of the pioneers, but instead of chopping down trees and building a log cabin, we go and raid a skip to bring back all the window frames, door frames, old buckets and anything else that has potential.

Nothing's wasted in the valleys and almost everything ends up being reused: this so-called new policy of recycling is old hat to seasoned allotment keepers, and we were doing it long before it become fashionable.

It seems strange to me that this isn't common practice elsewhere. At a Cardiff site that won the Allotment of the Year award, for example, you walk in and there's not a single building there. It's completely flat and the plotholders are not permitted to build a greenhouse or a shed or anything else. I found the same at Highgate in London, where we were filming *The Big Dig*: there's all these lovely town houses overlooking the site, so no one's allowed to build anything in case they spoil the view.

Fashions change, though, and there seem to be a lot of people giving their back gardens a makeover who are keen to get rid of their aluminium greenhouses, because they're upgrading or perhaps building a conservatory instead. The free papers regularly carry advertisements offering them, for nothing, provided you dismantle and collect them yourself, and there's a new influx of these on the plots. They look a lot neater but somehow lack the character of the old shanties, and I suspect I shall keep mine the way it is, with its sash windows, corrugated plastic roof and an entrance through somebody's old internal door with a large glass window in it.

What amazes me is where these sheds and greenhouses are often sited. We'll say, 'Don't build there because you'll cast a large part of your plot in shade. Put it at the other end instead.' But they're always built where they're just a step off the main path because that's more convenient. And they tend to have the sun full on the building, which means several yards of good soil are in shade for most of the day.

There's almost no plot up there now that hasn't got a

greenhouse or a shed, and they're often large structures. The greenhouses are generally used just to grow seedlings and tomatoes, sometimes fifteen or twenty plants that produce massive amounts of fruit. And the sheds are used as stores, of course – or at least they were at first.

Once bottled gas became available, someone had the bright idea of bringing up a small stove so they could boil a kettle and make a cup of tea or coffee or sometimes a mug of soup. If you did that you could spend a whole day there and look after yourself quite comfortably.

The next step was to start cooking food. People would bring a piece of meat with them, go out on the plot and gather fresh vegetables, put all these ingredients in a pot and make a fresh broth. While they were gardening in the morning, this would be bubbling away in the shed for whenever they were ready to break for lunch.

And then Albie started making coffee in his greenhouse, where he had a two-ring stove. One morning I was working away and suddenly I heard a shout: 'You want a coffee, Terry?' It was just what I needed. His plot's just across the path from mine and he had a couple of seats in there, so we sat down and relaxed for quite a while over coffee and biscuits.

A coffee break became a regular thing. Very soon other people began to join us, and in the end there'd be four or five of us gathering in his greenhouse. The stove would be on, the chat would flow and it was great. Once again allotmenteers are at the forefront of progress: Albie set the trend, Starbucks and Costa followed!

Then Rhys, who had a bigger stove in his shed and two big patio doors that you could open right up, started bringing up bacon, bread, tomatoes out of the greenhouse and some mush-rooms, and would cook breakfast. So we had a coffee shop *and* a café where you could meet for bacon sandwiches or a full mid-morning breakfast.

People began spending longer and longer up on the plots, not necessarily gardening but talking, eating and drinking, and that has changed the whole atmosphere. Instead of being an intensive work session, a visit to the allotment has become an important social event.

Some time before Albie's coffee bar started up, there used to be a wine club at the far side of the allotments where four or five members met regularly. They would gather wild crops like elderflowers or blackberries and brew their own wine in a shed belonging to one of them. On a Sunday night you would find these guys sitting outside this shed on a big long bench in the evening sunshine, enjoying the view up the valley and sampling their wine.

One Sunday evening while I was still a working man, I went up there to do the watering and took Anthea along for the ride and a stroll through the allotments afterwards. These guys were sitting there in the sun, and greeted Anthea politely (allotment holders are *always* well-mannered).

'Mrs Walton,' one of them said, 'would you like a glass of wine?'

She thought about it and then said yes, she would.

He went into the shed, fetched a wine glass from the stock he kept on a shelf, rinsed it out in his water barrel (which disturbed all the mosquito larvae) and then poured out this glass of wine. They didn't go in for the refinement of filtering their wine, so it came out somewhat murky.

I remember the look on Anthea's face as this brown, cloudy nectar was presented to her. She took a cautious sip, said, 'That's nice,' and drank it all down quickly to avoid prolonging the experience. But she wasn't used to home-made brews, and this was stronger than she had expected. With the heat and the sunshine, her legs began to feel heavy. Seeing how quickly she had drunk her wine, they asked if she'd like another glass, but she politely declined. We sat there chatting with them until the sun had finally set, and returned home with Anthea in a distinctly happy mood. She suffered no long-term effects.

We never did discover the identity of that amber nectar, and perhaps it was wise not to enquire: ignorance can often be bliss! That wine club continued for many years and eventually closed only when a couple of the members became too old to work on the allotment.

Several distinctive social groups now gather regularly up on the plots, which has enlivened things no end. It increases the popularity of the place, and people tend to stay longer instead of just doing their chores and leaving. Right throughout the year there's always someone around now, which never used to happen, especially during the winter. And that's good for site security, of course.

This is why people are reluctant to change allotments nowadays. They have become more attached to their plots, and don't want to give up their little bit of heaven to move closer to the gate. Thirty or forty years ago, when there were no fixed assets and it was more attractive to be where it was easier to bring in and take out whatever you needed, no. 1 plot was the ultimate goal of every member.

Recently it took me years to let no. 1 for any length of time. We did allow newcomers to have it because nobody else wanted it, but that didn't work out and as time went on the plot became quite scruffy. I finally managed to let it in 2006 to someone who immediately started building a greenhouse, something it lacked, and we are keeping our fingers crossed.

Even though some attitudes have changed with the more

relaxed regime, the choice of crops grown is still very basic and conservative. There might be a wider repertoire of seed varieties, but few people grow unusual vegetables and most concentrate on the same staples I grew in the fifties and sixties. Potatoes, cabbages and beans are grown in huge quantities. Few tend even to grow things like carrots and beetroot, seeds that are sown directly into the ground, perhaps because it's a little more complicated and needs more skill. And the rhubarb you used to see everywhere in the fifties because it was so dependable, giving you several months of rhubarb tarts and crumbles, is nowhere near as popular now.

Apart from about five or six of us who were there in the seventies, there are no really long-standing gardeners on the allotments now. People have been coming and going all the time, mainly going until the latter half of the eighties when the organic movement was gaining momentum and people began to look at growing their own again on a small scale. I suspect *The Good Life* series on television helped, making people think maybe they could do the same themselves.

After that, gardening became fashionable. There was this big upturn in people wanting to grow their own, a lot more people on television were plugging it, and suddenly it seemed that everybody wanted an allotment. It was back in favour once more, just like in the fifties. Even a programme like *Ground Force* helped: it might not have been about growing vegetables but it did make more people see the outdoors as a part of their life.

Perhaps this is why in the last twenty years we've taken in new members who are more builders than gardeners, at least initially. The first thing anybody does when they take on a plot now is build something, instead of turning the ground over and getting crops in. Even if there's already a shed and greenhouse, they'll install edging or divide their plots into smaller beds with more fixed paths. The hard landscaping comes first, and sometimes there can be more paths than arable land in the end. Perhaps it's the 'garden makeover' influence spreading from the back garden on to the plots.

I sometimes wonder if gardening programmes these days are getting a little too sophisticated, plugging grand landscape designs and letting the Latin names of exotic shrubs roll off their tongues, when many gardeners still just grow annuals in the front garden and vegetables out the back, with no space for an ambitious herbaceous border.

I think there's a need on television for more information on basic vegetable gardening, perhaps ten or fifteen minutes in a show every week during the growing season explaining what you should be doing now on the veg plot. It's not enough to look at the seed packet and follow the advice there because conditions may not be right on the ground. This is something I try to address on air whenever I can.

In the last few years we've been getting a lot more active support from our local council, partly because of this growing demand for allotments and also because of the media attention. They installed drainage pipes down the main road through the allotments, resurfaced it with hardcore, and then added a turning place so that plotholders can bring their cars right in, turn round and drive back out. This avoids the difficult manoeuvre of reversing out past all the obstacles at the ends of plots. In addition they excavated some waste ground outside the allotments to create a car park for members.

The Jeremy Vine Show seems to have put the Rhondda on the map now that we broadcast from there every two weeks. There have also been various television programmes, and when the camera on the plot catches the surrounding scenery, which, especially in the middle of the summer, is absolutely outstanding, it must convince people the Rhondda is more than just industrial history.

I like to think the threat to our allotments that alarmed us when interest was declining has now disappeared. There's a growing demand everywhere for plots, even pressure to increase their numbers, and this may persuade some authorities to think again about sites as a vital amenity rather than let them go for development just because of the pound signs waving before their eyes. I'm convinced allotments generally, and ours in particular, have a good future.

Certainly the calibre and variety of recent incomers give me grounds for hope. They're bringing in some new ideas and an injection of enthusiasm. Take Keith and his wife Jean. They are in their sixties, keen gardeners who have moved to the valleys from Swindon. Keith's allotment has become more of a leisure garden than a conventional plot. He grows quite a lot of vegetables, but he's also got apples and other top-fruit trees – things that were rarely planted in the old days – as well as an inviting bench, a patch of lawn and a pond. It's great, looks tidy and aesthetically pleasing, and is the kind of plan our committee is happy to accept.

Then there's Carl, who is in his thirties and just finishing long service in the army. He's a more traditional vegetable grower: plenty of beans, cabbages and the various root crops, but nothing exotic, exactly as it used to be long ago. There's also our well-known inventor, Russell Vaughan, who has seen the light and 'gone biodynamic'. He gardens according to the phases of the moon and uses a special calendar which tells him on what days to plant and which to avoid.

Roger has been a member since way back in the seventies and, like the rest of 'the '70s club' (as we call the elite few who have survived allotment gardening for thirty or more years), has gardened on many different plots in his quest to get closer to the gate. His allotment is one of the best on the site for tidiness and layout, with flowering shrubs and trellis laden with clematis among the areas devoted to vegetables.

And there's a special plot used by the local school for children with learning difficulties. That started a few years back when Jim Sullivan, a community policeman, was looking for somewhere safe so that the children could be outside in the fresh air. He approached several allotment sites that weren't interested at all or were concerned about the practicalities of having these kids around. Then he came to see us and was quite shocked when we said yes, no problem at all. A lot of our members help out and it's good to see how much enjoyment the kids derive from getting their hands dirty and seeing things grow. They come up during school hours, other people come in and help on some of the other days of the week, and the plot is really beginning to take shape.

The big problem they have – common to most school gardens – is that the summer term finishes about the third week of July and they then have the whole of August off, just when the crops are coming along nicely. There's nobody there in the holidays to do a bit of routine work and harvest the produce, which is a shame because they've all worked hard up until then. Most of the produce goes to waste as plotholders never go on to other plots without permission.

All in all, the allotments are a lively place to be these days.

But the changes that have occurred haven't eroded some of the typical allotment attitudes, such as the old-fashioned respect and helpfulness members have traditionally shown towards one another. It must have something to do with sharing a good cause and working outdoors with plants and the soil. Even today, when all around us common courtesy seems to be on the wane, no self-respecting plotholder would dream of charging another plotholder for produce. Members tend to combine in natural groups who share any surplus plants or produce among themselves.

The habit of sharing means you don't have to be quite so concerned about continuity and range of produce on your own plot. Most of us grow more than enough of something for our own needs, especially lettuces, cabbages, beans and other stuff that doesn't keep too well, and there'll be a surplus to share with others. Someone will always be able to give you something if you run out. It's the same with tomatoes. I always end up growing more than enough plants for my purposes, so I can supply Albie and Nuts with some of those left over. Then, come midsummer, Nuts will usually give me a large carrier bag full of tomatoes because he's got more than he needs, and I bring them home for Anthea to make lots of soup and tomato chutney. I don't charge anything for the plants in the first place, but I get something in return later which is of more value to me than money.

Sometimes you try to grow something that fails miserably – these things happen to the best of us – but not everybody's unsuccessful and you rarely find yourself going without. This doesn't happen so much with staples like potatoes or onions, because these are grown for store and people don't tend to give them away unless you've had a real disaster, but more perishable crops are always readily exchanged between groups of plotholders. They would only be wasted otherwise, and why watch a cabbage or a lettuce go to seed if there's somebody who can use it?

Again, some people simply don't grow certain things. Albie, for example, never sows his own beetroot, but he's usually the first among us to pick runner beans, so I'll usually get a feed of beans earlier than I would off my own, and in return I'll give him a few bunches of my beetroot throughout the summer. Because my beans will tend to run on a week or two later than his, he'll get some of those off me at the end of the season, when all his plants are exhausted.

Early beetroot

 I LIKE TO PULL a steady supply of beetroot through the season, and start the first batch extra early by sowing in pots.

A beetroot seed is a little knobbly brown thing that is in fact a capsule containing several seeds. Come early March I put two or three of these capsules in a small pot, about 1½ in (4 cm) in diameter by 2 in (5 cm) deep, and keep these in the greenhouse to germinate and grow on. I do about twenty to twenty-five of these pots, thinning the seedlings to leave three to four beetroot plants in each. In early May I transplant the complete potfuls outdoors. I start pulling the roots when they're not much bigger than a ping-pong ball, and use them as my first early beetroot. The rest I leave to grow to roughly the size of a tennis ball, and they'll be my second harvest.

All the other beetroot sowings go straight in the ground, because they are fairly easy to grow and for some reason largely trouble-free – no aphids, no beetles, and even a slug will only occasionally nibble at a seedling leaf.

So there's a lot of swapping of vegetables going on between all the various plotholders in their small self-help groups. This sometimes surprises newcomers in their first year or two, before they've mastered the art and started producing steadily for themselves. We can all sympathize – we've been there ourselves once – and always give them something to take home. Then when they go out of the gate they're taking some locally grown produce with them, and also an understanding of the cooperative way life goes on here, which is probably more valuable in the long term.

Plants are regularly exchanged, especially young transplants like cabbages, lettuces or Brussels sprouts, because you always raise more than you want, whereas new plotholders may not be familiar with how to plan far ahead or raise their own seedlings. Surplus onion sets or seed potatoes get shared out in the same way.

It's all part of the ancient custom of barter, and no money ever changes hands. It's the same with practical help: as I said before, if someone's ill, a neighbouring member will often do the plot for him and take produce to the house. People help you out if you've got a problem or simply water the plot for you if you can't get there. Help and cooperation on the plots is an allotment tradition.

The exchange system even works with outsiders who come to the allotments looking for surplus crops, and over the years I've gone home with all sorts of weird and wonderful swaps. Someone who keeps chickens on the top plots will often come down looking for some veg, and you'll probably get a dozen new-laid eggs in return. There's a local angler who fishes for rainbow trout in a lake near here, and he often comes up for two or three pounds of beans. He'll ask, 'How much is that?' and of course you say, 'Oh, don't worry about it.' The next time he turns up he'll usually bring a fat, freshly gutted trout.

Wayne is a long-term plotholder, one of the '70s club, and after many moves he now tends the plot next to me, third in from the gate. He's an excellent gardener but has suffered ill health in recent years and undergone several serious operations, all of which makes gardening a bit of a trial. I do as much as I can to help him, and sometimes I've planted his plot and harvested produce when the crops are ready. Now Wayne's wife makes her own bread, and when I call in at their house to drop off stuff from the plot, I always come back with a piping hot, home-baked loaf.

We had someone there who never grew marrows – I don't know why, because they're so simple – but he always liked to make marrow rum. He'd ask me, if I had any spare marrows, to save them for him, and so I used to grow a couple of reasonable-sized specimens and give him those. In due course I'd receive two bottles of marrow rum in return.

Another example is Russell, who we all call 'Nuts' because he used to go around with a pocketful of peanuts that he was forever picking at. He's an inventive gardener who can happily spend three hours making some special tool to save himself twenty minutes' work. He grows everything in square pots, because he reckons that saves space and the plants grow better than in round pots, and so he made himself a square dibber for transplanting all those square rootballs to holes of the right shape. When he wants to net his cabbages against the pigeons, he puts a series of canes in the ground and then goes to Porthcawl at the end of the season to buy up their used tennis balls cheaply. He splits these with a Stanley knife and fits them over the ends of the canes, so the net will sit nicely without getting caught.

Whatever you want, Nuts has got it somewhere in his shed, whether it's screws, nails or washers, in any particular size you name. And he's a great collector of gadgets for every job under the sun. He's got a semi-automatic riddle for sieving soil (which the rest of us don't do – we use compost) and a pump for getting water out of barrels, whereas the rest of us simply siphon it out. He just has to have a special tool for everything. He used to be a toolmaker, so it figures.

One year Nuts's veg had failed so some of us had been giving him our surplus. He regularly goes out shooting and he came in one day with a brace of partridge for me and another brace for Albie. I didn't know what to do with them – they're not something I'm familiar with – so he took them away and prepared them, and then brought them back all trussed and ready for cooking.

There's an elderly lady living nearby, the widow of a man who used to teach me when I was at school, and she will often come over on a Sunday morning to see if we've got any spare runner beans for her dinner. She always brings a small tin of Welsh cakes, freshly cooked, to trade in exchange, and we keep these to have with our coffee throughout the week. So even outsiders join in with the allotment barter system.

Plotholders seldom ask for anything outright, though. The usual opening gambit is to remark casually, 'Oh, those cabbages are looking nice then,' or 'You seem to have a lot of tomatoes in there!' Never a direct 'Can you spare me some of them?' But you're cute enough to translate that as meaning they haven't got any of their own, and wouldn't mind some, please, if you've got any to spare.

One of the old unspoken rules is that you always deal face to face. Nobody goes on anyone else's plot without permission, so even if someone had told you to help yourself you wouldn't dream of doing so unless they were there. No one would go on your plot and cut or pick something if you weren't around.

The only thing you'll ever take from anybody else is water, and that's because it's free to all, running constantly out of the hillside. If they've got their hose connected up and running, you know you are at liberty to go and join your hose on to theirs to share the supply. But you wouldn't actually go and take produce. You never touch without being given.

That's one of the very few rules these days, and compared with my father's day there is a much more easy-going atmosphere now, and it's got better and better as the years have gone on. The majority of us are not working any more, so that probably contributes, but even when I started quite a few members had retired and it was never as friendly and relaxed as now.

I find since I've retired that I can go up to the plot sometimes and wonder exactly what I've done all day. This applies in foul conditions as much as fair. A lot more people seem to turn up as usual nowadays in inclement weather, whereas before if it was raining there was simply no point in going; you couldn't do anything. Now you can always do a bit of work in your greenhouse as well as spending an hour or two chatting in the shed.

It's far more of a community than ever before, and you very rarely walk in and find the place empty. There's usually someone in there from early morning until sundown, depending on their habits: some people like to go at half five in the morning to enjoy three or four hours before the sun is up fully, whereas others prefer to be there in the early evening and stay until the sun goes down, or even later.

Terry's Tip for October

A pond on the plot

TRY TO FIND ROOM on your allotment for a pond. It doesn't have to be large. You can direct the overflow from your greenhouse water butts there to keep it topped up, and you'll find it hosts all kinds of wildlife that will feed on various garden pests and help you control them without using any poisons.

Among the first allies a pond will usually attract are frogs and toads, which feed voraciously on slugs and, if conditions are right, will produce masses of spawn in spring to increase their populations. You can always tell one kind from the other: frogspawn looks like masses of transparent jelly studded with black dots, which are the eggs, whereas toadspawn forms in long floating ribbons.

It always amazes me where creatures come from once you install a pond. You may never see frogs or toads on a plot, but construct a pond and they very soon colonize it. Newts appear from under moist stones, and beetles fly in before you've even finished filling it with water.

The aim is to attract as many pest predators as possible to help you in the organic approach to controlling pests. Birds, for example, will enjoy the benefits of a handy oasis, flying down to drink at the watering hole and then lingering in the surroundings to catch the odd aphid or two.

Anthea's Recipe for October

Tomato Relish

IKE SOME OTHER CROPS, tomatoes tend to ripen in great flushes once the plants are up to speed. One way of using the surplus is to skin and purée the fruit for freezing, to add to soups and stews throughout the year. This is another suggestion, which transforms tomatoes into a warming relish to remind you of summer on a cold winter's day.

- 4 lb (1.8 kg) ripe tomatoes
- 2 lb (900 g) sugar
- 2 large onions
- 1 pint (600 ml) malt vinegar
- 5 tbsp plain flour
- 2 heaped tsp curry powder
- 2 heaped tsp mustard
- 3 oz (85 g) salt

Skin and chop the tomatoes and onions, sprinkle with salt and leave in a bowl overnight.

Next day drain off and discard the liquid, put the vegetables in a pan and cover with vinegar. Boil for 5 mins.

Blend flour and curry powder with enough vinegar to make a smooth paste. Add this and the sugar to the contents of the pan.

Bring back to the boil and simmer gently for 1 hour, stirring until the contents reduce to form a relish.

CHAPTER ELEVEN

Pumpkins at Large

EVEN THOUGH THE gardening press and other media are always on the lookout for new ideas to attract readers' interest, most of the crops grown on the allotments remain the same as they have been for decades, even generations. This has much to do with the natural conservatism of Rhondda gardeners that I've already mentioned, but there's also sound common sense behind it. At its heart allotment gardening is all about growing food, and this means ensuring a good supply of the staples that you depend on from day to day.

We might not live in a subsistence economy any more, but we've still got to eat. That's the top priority, but it doesn't have to exclude experiment and adventure, even perhaps some fun. Now 'fun' is not a word that would have been used on allotments way back, but many people are thinking about their leisure a lot more now, rather than concentrating on just being providers.

I still grow for the wholesome flavour of my own fresh food and to know where it's coming from, but people are being tempted by the exotics and the more unusual ingredients for adding to dishes, because they've got used to finding them in supermarkets. And these days I'm getting more and more keen to try something new as well. I was totally conservative earlier on, but now there's just the two of us to feed, as opposed to a growing family, I feel I can spare a bit of ground for novelties, provided I'm still getting an adequate supply of what I need to live on for most of the year.

The media interest has been a huge encouragement, because there's obviously a professional concern that audiences don't want to hear every year only about the standard vegetables which I grow. So over the past few seasons I have expanded my range of crops and methods, and I'm finding that exploring them adds a little spice to allotment life. Rather like swimming, once you dip your toe in you find it's not so bad after all.

The first big change for me came with marriage and the arrival of children, and the need to expand from a concentrated season of commercial vegetables to a wider range of food crops to feed us throughout the year. But family circumstances are constantly evolving. As recently as the late nineties the structure of the Walton household changed again. In July 1998 our younger son, Andrew, got married to his long-term girlfriend, Sarah. This event was followed in March 1999 by the wedding of his brother, Anthony, to Alison.

Thus in a short space of time the household shrank to just the pair of us once more. This led to complications at meal times as Anthea adjusted to feeding two after so many years of catering for four, and I found I was growing too much. With time this change resolved itself, and now that both sons live within a short distance of us there are two extra households dependent on allotment produce. The circle of life keeps on turning and, as I've always said, if you stand still long enough, everything catches up with you.

Then there was my father's new greenhouse, which introduced me to growing tomatoes and cucumbers under glass, something I've done every year since. In the last six years I've grown peppers as well, because we tend to eat a lot of them. What deterred me from growing them before was their reputation for attracting greenhouse whiteflies. These can be a real nuisance and are difficult to avoid, although I've found that planting marigolds (*Tagetes* varieties) with the peppers helps enormously to deter the pests from settling into the crop in the first place.

This is one kind of companion planting that I find does work, perhaps because of the closed environment under glass. I don't subscribe very much to companion planting ideas outdoors, however, where conditions are more variable. I've tried growing carrots between rows of onions, for example, without any success: I'm convinced that the carrot fly, although a very small creature, must have a fair-sized nose and would probably find the carrots no matter how strong the scent of onions.

It always amuses me when you buy some of these so-called root fly-resistant carrots, because the seed packets will sometimes advise you to grow them near a non-resistant type. That suggests to me that they are in fact only slightly more resistant than the ordinary kinds, and you should still grow these as a sacrificial crop which, given the choice, the flies will attack first. Another kind of companion planting, perhaps?

Some pungent herbs act as deterrents, but their effect is only partial. Like all other organisms, pests evolve and adapt, and eventually find a way round your schemes.

A relatively new idea, which we spotted while recording a television show recently on some other allotments and which some of us have since tried, is growing carrots in large bins some 3 ft (90 cm) above the ground. Over our two seasons of trials there's been no carrot root fly whatsoever on some really nice clean roots, and I've been sufficiently impressed to have a go myself. I put some stones in the bottom to act as drainage, add the compost mix emptied out of the greenhouse border to three-quarters full, and then top up with fresh growbag compost to give the seeds a good start.

Something I'm trying to develop now is a natural form of slug and snail control, always a challenge for organic gardeners. We don't have any song thrushes these days, but we do have a lot of local frogs up on the mountain behind us and in the wild, abandoned area that flourishes in the top corner.

A few years ago, when somebody gave me an old empty drum, I decided to install a pond on my allotment – only about 5 ft (1.5 m) across but large enough to satisfy frogs, which only need water at breeding time. I sank the drum to its rim in the ground, filled it with water and stocked it with some oxygenating and aquatic plants and some frogspawn, all from my pond at home. To my surprise and delight, frogs spawned in there of their own accord in 2005 and again the following spring, so they've obviously established themselves. Just behind the pond there's a corrugated zinc barrier and my thicket of blackberries, which I leave a little wild to provide natural hiding places for the frogs.

Feeding the frogs

SOME TIME AROUND JULY, when the new generation of little frogs are starting to develop but are not yet ready to leave my pond, I combine some simple pest control with feeding them up for their venture into the wider world.

I grow a lot of sweet peas, and these are like magnets to aphids, which always seem to go for the growing tips. I like to spend a nice summer's evening going round the plants and collecting up these aphids. All I do is bend the flexible growing tip into a paper bag, give it a good tap with my finger, and all the aphids fall in because they don't cling on very tightly.

Then I go down and scatter them on the surface of the pond to feed the baby frogs, which immediately start gobbling them all down. That way the frogs have a good body-building diet for several weeks before they leave (and hopefully get the taste for aphids as well) – if they're fat and robust they're more likely to survive the winter. And I keep my sweet peas clean with very little effort and no poisons.

Making that pond was a conscious part of finding an alternative means of pest control, although I've always carried a flag for wildlife and have never supported killing a rabbit or disturbing a hedgehog or badger, for example. To me these are simply a part of the natural world with their own roles to play in the balance of life, something that intervention by man usually upsets.

A fox, for example, can live quite happily in the country and adjusts its own numbers according to the amount of food that's available. It will help control the rabbit population because there's a natural food chain and relationship there. But when man starts getting involved, an imbalance sets in, and these creatures get driven into urban areas where they thrive completely unnaturally. You might see a nice bushy-tailed fox walking through a suburban garden, but that's not where it's supposed to be. You shouldn't have foxes living under your shed in an urban area, eating out of dustbins instead of hunting rabbits. Such foxes are no longer predators but scavengers.

I've got mixed feelings about some kinds of wildlife though, especially since the gardener's friend, the humble honey bee, seems to have made me its enemy. It all began during an hour-long special of *The Jeremy Vine Show* that I shared with Jimmy Doherty (he of *Jimmy's Farm* fame). We were discussing the merits of keeping bees and I made a plea on air for some beehives on the allotment. Laura and Anthony, a local couple and both enthusiastic beekeepers, got in touch with me and offered to put two hives on our plots. I went to visit them and we did a broadcast, with them explaining the benefits of keeping bees.

I was appropriately kitted out from head to toe in a protective suit, including a face veil, and felt perfectly safe when they opened up their hives. While I was looking inside one of them and talking away to Jeremy with the mobile pressed to my ear over the veil (which stretched it tight across my nose), I spotted a bee landing on the bridge of my nose and starting to crawl downwards. It reached the tip and then promptly committed hara-kiri by stinging the end of my nose.

I continued talking on air as though nothing had happened, even though my eyes were streaming and my nose running like a tap – what a pro!

By the time I got home my rather bulbous red nose made me look like a circus clown. And I took plenty of stick at the pub that night, with predictable comments like 'Good job it's not Christmas, you could stand in for Rudolph.'

To add insult to injury, I was doing the show live with Laura two weeks later, after the bees had been installed on the allotment, and we both went up to have a look at the hives, just to see if the bees were working. No need for safety gear this time. We were standing close by, explaining to Jeremy how the bees seemed to have settled down, when two of them decided to sting me for no reason at all, one on the chin and the other on my neck. By the evening I looked like a bad case of mumps. In future I think I'll keep a wary distance.

When I went organic in the eighties, I started exploring other vegetable varieties, because some are more successful than others if you're doing without artificial fertilizers and chemical pesticides. I found I couldn't better 'Boltardy' as a beetroot variety, although I did try some others, such as 'Crimson Globe'. I used to favour a carrot variety called 'Parano' which has disappeared from the catalogues and I am now trying 'Maestro' to see how that does on my ground. I've moved away from the short stubby kinds because my soil's become very deep with cultivation and they don't produce so much crop for the space they take.

Onion sets have been 'Sturon' for as long as I can remember, and I think the best shallot is still 'Golden Gourmet'. My peas tend to be 'Kelvedon Wonder', a fine old early and late variety with good natural resistance to mildew, but I grow '(Hurst's) Greenshaft' for maincrops. I'm a little more adventurous with runner beans, which were always 'Scarlet Emperor', and now I grow 'Polestar' or 'Lady Di', which I find give good-size beans and do not tend to become tough and stringy even towards the end of the season.

Under glass I grow 'Bella' or 'Petite' cucumbers, both of them short female-only hybrids, because we've learned that it is better to have a small cucumber you can eat in one meal than to grow the traditional long ones which end up going to waste in the fridge. And my sweet peppers are usually 'Gypsy' these days, because they turn red extremely easily: a lot of varieties go through the natural cycle from green to light orange and then red, and some of them take ages, but 'Gypsy' finishes ripening very quickly.

After many years of growing first 'Moneymaker' and then 'Alicante' as my standard tomato variety, I've settled on 'Shirley', a well-tried kind which as a hybrid is more expensive to buy as seed but seems to be resistant to most problems and does extremely well for me. I like to grow a couple of 'Gardener's Delight' too because they crop well right through until November, and you get a good steady harvest of cherry-size fruit on huge trusses. I don't grow any tomatoes outdoors because they're a waste of time in our short growing season.

Ideally I'd grow a good beefsteak tomato too, but even one plant takes up a lot of room. In an average-size greenhouse it's hard to find space for more than a few tomatoes, three cucumbers and at least a dozen pepper plants. They always reckon you should have separate houses for tomatoes and cucumbers, because of their different preferences for heat and humidity, but I've always grown them together in the same greenhouse and never had problems. If you haven't got the luxury of ample space, you make do without.

I use the extreme corners of the greenhouse for the

cucumbers, one inside the door and one in each back corner, so they may get more humidity trapped in the corners, although strangely the one in the doorway, which is the coolest place, has given the greatest crop before now.

I don't grow greenhouse crops in growbags because I like my plants to have a footing in the ground, but I do use their contents as one of the cheapest sources of potting compost. When I remake the greenhouse borders every two years, I spread some well-rotted manure on the bottom, fill the beds from my bins of home-made compost and then spread the contents of a couple of growbags on the top, and everything does very well in that without the water stress they could experience growing in bags.

These indoor crops have to be sown early, in my heated greenhouse in the back garden or in the airing cupboard (thanks, Anthea!), because they need a long growing season to crop. A slightly later sowing will often catch up and you can delay things a bit until it's warm enough to sow on a windowsill or even on the staging in an unheated greenhouse.

But there comes a point beyond which it's too late. A seed takes however long it needs to germinate, grow and yield, and if you're too late starting the cycle you could find yourself into August before you know it, when the majority of stuff has stopped growing in the shortening days, and if you do manage to harvest a crop it will be greatly reduced.

The amount of leeway you have with conditions like the number of days to maturity a plant needs is often limited, and you need to match timing and variety to the particular nature of the locality and typical climate. This applies very much to sweetcorn, which wants plenty of sun and heat in August to do well, and plants need to be flowering and setting by then.

I've been growing sweetcorn for nearly a decade. The first

year I grew a standard large variety, but ended up with half-filled cobs, so the following year I tried 'Mini-pop', which is a small type with sweet immature cobs used in stir-fries and eaten raw in salads. They don't need pollinating, you harvest them before the tassel withers on the cob, and they're so tiny that you usually get three or four per stem.

They did extremely well for me (and have done ever since). The next year someone offered me half a dozen sweetcorn plants that were going spare, and I got those in just after the last frosts, which gave them the maximum growing season outdoors. The result was six cracking full-size cobs, persuading me to go back to growing those again. The variety was 'Sundance', which matures early, a great asset in our indifferent Welsh summers. The plants are best grown in rich, fertile soil in squares to ensure the cobs are pollinated, because this depends for success on the wind blowing the pollen from the top of the plant on to the tassels of the immature cobs below and on adjacent plants.

You have to make full preparations when the cobs are ready for picking (shrivelled tassels are a good indication). The cobs need to be cooked and eaten, or frozen, almost immediately after harvest because the sugar starts changing to starch very quickly – after only twenty minutes, some authorities say. So the sooner you eat them, the sweeter they are. They also need plenty of space and careful positioning because they can be very tall and cast a lot of shadow over their neighbours.

One season recently I tried to get a second, late crop of 'new' potatoes. I had seen seed tubers advertised that had been kept refrigerated for late planting, and thought I'd have a go. I planted them in August, they soon came up and looked reasonably good, and there were no late frosts to cause any problems. But by the end of September, when the days were becoming shorter and cooler, the plants started to turn yellow so I dug them out. I think the size of the potatoes I harvested was significantly smaller than those I put in, and we had enough for just one meal.

Again this might be something to do with the length of our growing season, which always makes me cautious about trying too many glamorous or unfamiliar new varieties. With potatoes I tend to grow largely the same ones year in, year out. I might try an odd novelty now and again but only as a small sample, just to see what it's like. To be sure of results I keep mainly to my standard early, second crop and maincrop kinds. I tend to grow a lot of 'Arran Pilot' as my early, although I did try 'Pentland Javelin', which is a nice shape but didn't crop as heavily as 'Pilot'.

I started growing 'Charlotte' a few years ago when it became the 'in' potato, and that does quite well for me as a second early. But I find that 'Kestrel' is one of the best for a follow-on crop, an attractive potato with a lovely shape and tiny little purple eyes. Remember, though, that it's very difficult to grow maincrop potatoes in sufficient quantities to become self-sufficient, because they're big plants and take up a tremendous amount of allotment space.

In 2005 the adventurous gardener came out in me again when I tried a completely new maincrop potato that I saw advertised in a daily paper. It was called 'Sarpo', a Hungarian variety that was said to be completely resistant to blight. They were very expensive – nearly £20 for just forty potatoes – but I thought, what the hell, I need to crack the blight problem, so why not indulge myself? So I sent for them, and I must admit I had my doubts when they arrived, because they looked totally insignificant considering their cost.

I planted them in mid-April, they took an age to come through, and I began to think those keel slugs of mine had probably enjoyed a very expensive meal. Eventually they appeared, though, and grew an enormous amount of foliage. They went through August into September without any tell-tale signs of blight, whereas other varieties around the plots had succumbed badly to the disease.

About the second week in September I couldn't contain my inquisitiveness any longer and had to dig up one of the plants to see what, if anything, was under that mass of green topgrowth. To my great surprise there was a very good crop down below – but alas, they were a red variety, which always attracts the little black keel slug (the one that lives under-ground and is hardest of all to defeat), and some holes were already appearing in the tubers. They all had to come out then, despite the fact there was probably two or three weeks' more growth left in them.

They certainly succeeded in proving their blight resistance, and the experiment confirmed that it's always worth trying something new. To avoid further heavy expense, I saved forty of my own tubers to trial again the following year.

In 2006 I tried growing overwintered onions from sets for the first time, starting them at the end of August 2005 with the aim of lifting in May just as the stored onions ran out. It was a very sharp winter, the coldest for ten years, so it was probably not a reliable trial. Although they made a lot of growth in the early part of the winter and looked well in April, there was still very little bulb at the base at the time when the previous year's onions hanging up in the shed were starting to sprout and needed using up.

This always happens once the weather turns warm in the spring, leaving a barren two months without any fresh onions

– getting a full twelve-month supply is difficult, and the over-wintered ones were supposed to fill that gap. But they needed to be on time, because by mid-July I could start using some of my green spring-sown crop.

However, despite the harsh winter making them mature later than I had hoped, I was able to pull onions just when we needed them. They were smaller than the spring-sown ones, but usable nonetheless, and sweeter in flavour, perhaps as a result of their struggle through the cold weather. Mission accomplished.

On the whole I don't think I've discovered anything that I wish I'd grown years ago, though. When I tried pak choi it bolted to seed, so I didn't even get a taste of that. Salsify was nice, with a delicate flavour like asparagus, but the roots were quite small and never made a significant size. I've never grown asparagus (although my father tried it, without success), because our soil tends to be too heavy and supports huge numbers of keel slugs which graze on the spears just below ground level.

One crop we really did enjoy without any reservations was the vast and unexpected supply of mushrooms which sprang up after we started using spent mushroom compost on the plot.

Back in the eighties people's tastes were changing and a lot more mushrooms were being used in the kitchen. New places began producing them to meet this demand, and not far away in the Vale of Glamorgan they were starting up at a phenomenal rate. The standard way to raise them there was to make up bags filled with a mixture of bracken, compost and a bit of lime, and grow the mushrooms on top in very long, steamy polytunnels. Vast amounts of used mushroom compost came out of these bags once the crop was finished, which became an embarrassment to the farms. Its use as an excellent soil improver hadn't caught on at that stage and so they were having difficulty getting rid of the stuff.

In desperation they started to get in touch with allotment societies. One contacted us and said they couldn't move for this enormous mountain of old compost in the yard, and were we interested? We said, 'Well, what's the deal?' And they explained they didn't want anything for the compost, they were so glad to get rid of it, and all we had to do was pay for the lorry to bring it across.

So there we were in the mid-eighties, with as much compost as the driver could get on the lorry – anything up to 300 bags or more – and all it cost us was a £40 tip plus petrol. There was enough for three of us to have 100 bags or more each, which was fantastic: for less than £15 you had as much as you could use, delivered to the door. This idea caught on around the allotments, until the guy was bringing four or five loads over to us, if not more.

We found the stuff was ideal for root vegetables such as parsnips, carrots and beetroots: they don't benefit from manuring, which makes them fork, but they certainly revelled in the friable, loamy-based soil you got after digging in mushroom compost. If you could turn it in during the autumn, by the time you came to plant you had a beautifully textured soil and grew some extremely clean roots. And it contained a small amount of lime, which was particularly beneficial for sweetening and lightening our naturally heavy, slightly acid soil.

As a really surprising bonus, particularly when you added some of this compost to the greenhouse borders or to the bean trench, there'd be copious supplies of mushrooms. Some days I could fill two or three carrier bags with them, so I had my money back in my crop, let alone in the lasting worth of the compost.

We were really enjoying this situation. The price began to creep up by the odd five or ten pounds, but for a few years a lorryload was still extremely good value split between three of us. And then some gardening programme or magazine extolled the virtues of mushroom compost as a soil improver, and suddenly people were queuing at the mushroom farm in their cars, paying something like 70p for a bag of compost *and* taking it away. Abruptly our deliveries ceased, and after that we had to find a van and fetch our supply ourselves. It was still worthwhile, however, and we continued to use and appreciate it as before.

But what's happened now, in the twenty-first century? Apparently Polish farmers can bring mushrooms into this country cheaper than people can grow them in Wales, and all the mushroom farms in Wales have had to shut down. In 2006, for the first time for years, we were unable to get a supply of mushroom compost from anywhere. That vast source of natural organic material has gone completely.

Sadly there isn't a convenient and affordable substitute for a full-size allotment. No one can afford to dig proprietary compost into that extent of ground, so all we can do now is go back to using manure and then grow roots the following year to mop up the residues. But the mushroom compost spoilt us, and the old traditional way of working seems less effective to us now.

A lot of the manure I do get is handy for the particularly greedy crops, like beans, potatoes and of course all the various squashes, which thrive on rich food. I used to grow marrows but I don't do that now my supplier of potent rum is no longer around, and instead I grow courgettes, harvesting them as small fruits and then leaving the last few to grow to the size of marrows. And the pumpkin I grow needs *at least* a couple of wheelbarrow loads to itself.

The trouble with pumpkins is that they're rampant plants and take up an enormous amount of space, especially when you are growing for size, as I do. One plant occupies a patch 24 ft (8 m) by about 8 or 9 ft (2.5 m) wide, which is a lot of allotment to give up. The pumpkin itself forms at least 8 ft (2.4 m) from the main stem, and then you need another 12 ft (3.5 m) or more growth beyond to ensure enough strong foliage to feed the fruit. And that's for just a single champion pumpkin.

It sounds extravagant, but it's fun and a bit of a challenge. It all started in 2003 when my daughter-in-law Alison gave me one of those kits for Christmas with odd seeds in: giant sunflowers and square tomatoes and that sort of thing. So to keep her amused I thought I'd try out all these things. Quite a few pumpkin seedlings came up. I chose the strongest and gave the rest away. I planted it at the top of the plot, not really knowing how much space it might cover.

Jeremy Vine took a particular interest in pumpkins that year, and mine became a focus on his programme. We watched the plant grow and flower, and I gave a regular report on its progress. Eventually a fruit set and started to form. I described this pumpkin to Jeremy and confidently told him, 'It's slightly smaller than a golf ball, so we're on our way, we're looking good.'

A fortnight later we did the next show, and I had to report, 'Disaster! This pumpkin, I went to look at it this morning, and it's hollow. A slug has eaten all the flesh.'

This was the same day that Jeremy Vine was doing an interview with John Major, the ex-Prime Minister. At the start, at noon, Jeremy announced, 'Today in the studio we have John Major talking about his life as the Prime Minister. And news just breaking from the adopted allotment: the slugs have eaten the pumpkin!' That made the press as well.

But I managed to get another to develop, and in the end I produced a pumpkin that year weighing 35 lb (16 kg).

During the same season I had been involved in my spare time with a local charity called Bobath, which worked on behalf of children with cerebral palsy. I rang them up and said, 'Look, I've got this 35 lb pumpkin here. Can you make some money out of it?'

'Oh yes, we'd love to have that,' they said, because of course it was now associated with the famous *Jeremy Vine Show*. So we got hold of a photograph of Jeremy for publicity, and the pumpkin ended up as the star of a Guess the Weight competition at the Hallowe'en Ball in a large hotel in Cardiff, with several hundred guests. Tickets were on sale at a pound a time, winner takes the pumpkin.

But when they did the raffle, found a winner and came to give out the prize, it was gone. Somebody had openly pinched the pumpkin and walked out of the hall with it. However, it had made several hundred pounds for the charity, which was great.

At some point on Jeremy's show I was talking about the pumpkin when a listener rang in to suggest that the best way to make it grow large would be to feed it on beer. When I mentioned this ploy at my local pub, the landlord said he'd keep me all the part-barrels of real ale. There is always a small amount of beer left in the barrel that cannot be pulled and he would pour all of this, together with the slops from the drip trays, into one barrel for me.

The following year Wayne on the plot next to mine was ill

and unable to look after his plot, and we decided I would tend it for a year and devote the bottom half to my own use. I sent off for special giant pumpkin seeds, supposed to grow anything up to 1,000 lb (450 kg) in weight. I sowed several of these, selected the best seedlings, and planted two on the neighbouring plot.

A fruit set and grew to a reasonable size. Then I started feeding it with the beer, and it got bigger and bigger until it was pretty huge. Then another one formed, a little further along the plant. I somehow felt sorry for this one and fed it in the same way, with the result that the main fruit stopped swelling while its rival grew larger still. I ended up with one monster and another that weighed about 80 lb (36 kg).

By then Hen Felin, the school for children with learning difficulties, had taken on their plot at the allotments, so I asked Jim, the community policeman, whether the school had any fund-raising days. Like most of these places they were always looking for extra funds, and when I mentioned my monster pumpkin they decided to do something special and make a profit from it.

The local press were told, and then the story made the Welsh national news, especially when the tale got round about how it was fed on beer. To make something of the weigh-in, we invited the local fire brigade to come and transport it for us.

The guys on the allotment couldn't believe their eyes when a fire tender pulled up outside the gate and all the firemen came in with a blue tarpaulin, which they carefully unrolled next to the pumpkin. We got one of the schoolchildren to cut it free: I gave him my knife and then together, very carefully, we severed the stem. With a fireman at each corner of the tarpaulin, the pumpkin was lifted out to the tender, and then we set off with three police cars to escort us to Llwynypia

Hospital where it was to be weighed on the patients' scales – there was nothing else big enough.

Our arrival there caused huge excitement, with patients and nurses gathering to find out why all these police cars and a fire tender had pulled up outside. And then the back opened up and out came this pumpkin, to be carted into the hospital, where it turned out to weigh 12½ stone (175 lb or nearly 80 kg).

Those schoolkids were very inventive. First they scoured out all the flesh to make various kinds of chutney, then they turned the shell into a giant Hallowe'en lamp and touted that round to make money, and they even collected all the seeds to sell in packets. In the end that pumpkin raised about £700 for the school.

The next year, 2005, I decided to have another go, and thought I'd grow my plants from some of these seeds. 'Oh yes,' the kids said when I asked if there were any spare. 'Yes, you can have a packet. That'll be a pound, sir.'

So I had to buy back my own seeds before I could begin.

A winning technique

I ALWAYS START GROWING my pumpkins by burying two good barrowloads of manure in a big pit and covering this with soil which I raise into a slight mound.

To produce a giant you need seeds from a giant. Those I sow are about as big as the average thumb. I plant two with their pointed ends downwards in good seed compost in a pot that's at least 8 in (20 cm) in →

diameter. Germination can be spectacular, because the seed leaves muscle their way through the surface like an erupting volcano. If both emerge, I remove one and leave the other to grow on unchecked until it has six or seven leaves, and once cold weather is a distant memory it's planted out on the prepared site and watered in well.

I don't let any fruits set until one appears about 8 ft (2.4 m) from the main stem, to allow plenty of strong growth to feed it – and there's more manoeuvrability that far from the base, because any closer and the weight could pull the plant over. I hand pollinate the flowers because you can never be sure insects will fertilize them naturally. When the female flower (the one with a tiny fruit at the base) is fully open, I peel back the petals on the male to leave the stamens exposed and rub these over the centre of the female. If there are enough flowers open I might do two or three to make 100 per cent certain of success.

Once the first fruit has reached the size of a tennis ball, I take the rest off and surround the plant with half a dozen beer barrels (as a testament to its drinking prowess). Then I feed the plant with beer, 2–3 pints (1–1.5 litres) twice a day poured on about 18 in (45 cm) away – no closer or it might scorch the plant. I don't give any other feed because all that manure underground is enough for it to thrive on.

That year several of us on the allotments were involved in making the TV series called *The Big Dig* (shown on BBC2 in

2006). By now my pumpkins were becoming famous and the production team wanted me to grow another, this time competitively. The series was also focusing on another allotment site, in Highgate in London, where they had a Terry as well. So it was decided that my namesake there would compete with me to see who could grow the biggest pumpkin.

Well, the one I started just grew and grew, but I had to keep potting it on into a bigger container to fit the shooting schedule, when really it was long overdue for planting. That checked growth a bit and it finally went out into the ground later than I would have liked. But it still made 10½ stone (147 lb/67 kg) when it was weighed at the hospital, this time after a ceremonial collection by representatives of the four Welsh army regiments, who delivered it in an armoured car.

The pumpkin grown by Terry in Highgate failed to make the grade because he fed his on Pimm's. And Roger, one of the cast on our site, had a go and was ahead of me at one stage, but he started feeding his with cider, which burned it and made it rot. There's clearly no substitute for good local real ale.

It looks as though I'll be growing a large pumpkin every year now. It's a bit of frivolity really, but a good fund-raiser and a popular talking point when drip-feeding with beer is mentioned. People even come into the allotments to have a look at it, and the press like to follow its progress as we get into autumn. And when I say that it's real ale from the Barn the landlord's happy too, because he gets a well-deserved mention in the media.

In all honesty I'm not sure whether the beer actually helps, apart from creating an image in people's minds, especially when I tell them the plant has its own barrel with a pipe coming out to supply it with real ale every day of the week once it's a big lad. There might be a little feed in the yeast, perhaps, but I suspect the main benefit is simply a constant supply of ample moisture.

What started out almost as a joke seems to have become a tradition now, with benefits all round, and as a new season arrives I feel compelled to start again and try to better my results. I guess in many minds I'm now the pumpkin man, and the expectation's there each year that I'll grow another monster for everyone's amusement and to help swell the funds of a local charity.

And to think I told Tommy Parr, our showman, long ago that I wasn't the slightest bit interested in competitive growing!

Terry's Tip for November

Looking after brassicas

FORTUNATELY FOR ORGANIC GARDENERS you don't get too many diseases on allotments, especially if you keep the soil in good heart and regularly limed. Liming is important because most organic materials like manure and compost are naturally slightly acid, and calcium is always steadily leaching out, especially in wet areas like the valley, so that most soils tend to become acidic over the years.

Make a point of testing your soil with a simple pH test kit now and again. This will tell you whether it is acid or alkaline, and explain how to adjust it to suit what you want to grow. Most vegetables are happy with a pH range of 6.5–7.0, but the cabbage family prefer less acid conditions up to 7.2 or even higher (pH 7.5 has been shown to suppress clubroot, a real problem on acid soils). Liming the soil every autumn or spring before growing brassicas should keep the ground sweet enough.

We've got clubroot on our allotments, unfortunately, and I tend to control that with regular liming, plus extra precautions when planting out brassicas: I don't just make a little dibber hole and then push the earth back over the roots. Instead I use a trowel to make a fairly big hole, line this copiously with lime and then two-thirds fill it with fresh potting compost before fitting a pre-cut collar round the brassica stem to keep the cabbage fly from laying its eggs. Then I top up to surface level with more potting compost. This way each plant has a chance to make a fair-size root in sterilized soil before clubroot can take hold.

Anthea's Recipe for November

Sweet Pumpkin Cake

- 1 small pumpkin (about 1¼ lb/550–600 g), cut in wedges
- 9 fl oz (250 ml) sunflower oil
- 10 oz (300 g) muscovado sugar
- 8 oz (225 g) self-raising flour
- 3 large eggs
- 1 tsp baking soda
- 2 tsp ground ginger

Grease a 9 in (23 cm) cake tin generously with butter and dust with flour. Preheat the oven to 200°C/400°F/Gas Mark 6.

Put the pumpkin wedges on a tray and roast for 40 mins or until tender. Set aside to cool for 15 mins. Reduce oven temperature to 180°C/350°F/Gas Mark 4.

Scoop 9 oz (250 g) of flesh from the cooled pumpkin, and blend this to a purée.

Put oil and sugar in a large mixing bowl and whisk for 2 mins. Whisk in the eggs, one at a time.

Gradually fold in the flour, baking soda and ginger with a metal spoon. Add the pumpkin purée and stir.

Pour into the cake tin and bake for 40–45 mins, when the sides should start to shrink away from the tin. Turn out and cool on a wire rack.

Serve with vanilla ice cream.

CHAPTER TWELVE

Sharing the Adopted Allotment

A NEW FEATURE of life on the plot, which I'm just about getting used to, is that I can be working away up there when someone I've never seen before will come through the gate and ask, 'Where's Jeremy Vine's plot, then?'

'He hasn't got a plot,' I reply.

'I thought he had an allotment here,' they'll say. 'Who are you then?'

And I say, 'Terry. Terry Walton.'

'Oh, you're Jeremy Vine's gardener, aren't you?'

The Jeremy Vine Show seems to have a loyal following of listeners who love the allotment features and write in regularly to the show's message board. At first some of them were a little reluctant to believe that my bit actually goes out live: they suspected it was all pre-recorded and cut together in the studio. So it was agreed that a few of them, all regular 'posters' on the show's website, could come to the allotments to watch how it all happened.

Six visitors turned up one Friday lunchtime, arriving from west Wales, London and north-west England. They looked round the allotment, were introduced to Jeremy on air over the phone during the broadcast and then followed events as a live audience. Jeremy did his stuff in the studio and I did mine before their watching eyes, which proved conclusively that everything really is 100 per cent live, come rain, sun or snow, and that what they heard coming through their radios was actually happening.

In reality this can be a bit awkward at times because I have to create all the sound effects. I'm constantly nagging Jeremy to equip me with a hands-free device so that I don't have to hold the phone all the time. But he wants me either to put the handset down briefly or to do the gardening with it in my hand – which can make things somewhat difficult.

The point is that the phone captures the noises. An important aspect of radio broadcasting is that you have to make noise to create the ambience and paint a picture in the listeners' minds of what's happening. So I need to make sure they can actually hear all this rustling and banging and moving about to help them conjure up what I'm actually doing.

Some of the tasks are very difficult to do one-handed. There was the week I had my runner bean canes to put up, for example. It wasn't easy to push an 8 ft (2.4 m) cane deep into the ground with one hand while juggling the mobile with the other: the phone kept slipping down, the bundle of canes would follow and the canes would go in at the wrong angle. But I gather it made absolutely fantastic listening!

Another characteristic of live broadcasting is that you can't entirely predict what will happen until you do it. I was supposed to be digging my first early potatoes one summer, and I had to put the phone down briefly while I got the fork in place to lift the first tubers. The fork caught on something in the soil and instead of lifting the potatoes cleanly out of the ground it jerked up and buried the phone. Everybody could hear over their radios this thunderous sound of earth falling on to the phone, and I had to explain, 'Sorry, Jeremy, I've just buried you.'

Another time we were picking sweetcorn. I knew I'd have to pick a ripe cob, peel it and describe it. I thought I could talk while doing that, and jammed the phone in behind a corn cob next to the one I was going to pick.

So I went through all this rigmarole about finding and testing a ripe cob, picking and peeling it and everything else. What I didn't realize was that when I'd fixed the phone in position I had pressed the hold button.

All that our millions of listeners could hear on air was Jeremy's voice calling, 'Terry? Can't hear you, Terry. Where are you, Terry? Oh dear, we seem to have lost Terry!'

When I finished describing what I was doing, I picked up the phone and found it was on hold. I switched it back to live and said, 'Jeremy, you cut me off! What's happening there in the studio?' *That* surely must have proved the show was live.

Just before the General Election in 2005 Jeremy visited Scotland, Manchester and Cardiff in sequence for an election special, and while in Wales he came over to broadcast from the allotments. This was one of the few times the programme wasn't going straight out on the air: he had been in Manchester live on Thursday lunchtime, and then travelled down to get here early in the evening and record stuff to fit into his live Friday show from Cardiff.

We prepared a little surprise that evening. Down the side of the path were all my strawberries – lovely-looking plants, but not yet fruiting as it was still too early in May. So I rang up my son, who was coming with the rest of the family to meet Jeremy, and said, 'Do me a favour now. Call into Tesco's for me and pick up a punnet of strawberries.' When he brought them, I laid out all the fruits realistically on the plants.

They caught Jeremy's eye as soon as he arrived and started to look around. I said, 'Help yourself, they always crop early in the valleys.' But as he went to pick one, it rolled off the leaf and he realized at the last minute they weren't my own crop. 'You nearly had me there, Terry,' he said. Then he walked round the plot happily munching them while doing the commentary.

The four candidates for the Rhondda – Labour, Conservative, Plaid Cymru and Liberal Democrat – were invited to meet Jeremy here that evening for a political discussion. I remember it was a terrible night and pouring with rain while all four were standing on my plot. Jeremy pressed them on general party politics first of all, and then suddenly he brought them to a stop by saying, 'Now, if you got elected, what would you do for this allotment in the Rhondda?' Some were on the ball and gave useful answers – one was quick enough to say that tending an allotment fell in line with his party policy of a better, fitter society – but others were completely floored because the question was well outside their remit.

Broadcasts from the plot are always completely impromptu, although we have a little chat beforehand about the content. One spring I was growing salsify for the first time to give listeners an idea of how to do it. About three weeks after I'd sown it we were on air and Jeremy suddenly asked, 'Is the salsify coming yet, Terry?'

'I dunno,' I said. 'We'll walk down and have a look.' So I

talked my way down the path, and then said, 'Hang on, I'm going to run the phone over it now and see if it's up.' And I went back and forth over the ground with the phone, and said, 'Can you spot any of it yet?' (This is all make-believe: we pretend that the phone can see.)

'I don't even know what it looks like,' he protested, and I said, 'Well, neither do I, so that makes two of us!'

One November we had a very heavy fall of early snow. We'd planned the broadcast between us on the Wednesday, but by the time I went up on Friday morning there was a good 4 in (10 cm) of snow, and I had a devil of a job actually getting to the plot. And of course, when it snows everything ends up looking the same.

Anyway, once we were on air Jeremy asked, 'So what are we going to do today?'

I said, 'We're a bit stuck actually, because all I can see is one big white blanket of snow.'

So he said, 'Well, is the pond all right?' When I told him I couldn't even see it, he suggested we went to have a look. 'This is just a trick to get your own back for the strawberries, isn't it?' I said.

'I remember exactly where the pond is. Walk down the path, turn left at the bottom and then start to walk towards it,' he told me. 'Can you see it?'

'No, I *can't* see it.'

'Well, keep walking.'

'If I keep walking, I'll end up falling in.'

I went gently forward, tapping the snow and waving my mobile around like a camera as I described the scene for the listener, until I finally felt the edge of the pond ahead. I made loud crunching and splashing sounds, and said, 'Smack! I've found the pond now, Jeremy, but I haven't fallen in it.'

These stunts are all important on radio to fix the scene in the mind, and each programme needs at least two or three topics like this with live noise when you're describing what is actually happening here on an allotment through a mobile phone.

The programme evolved, because we had to think of something different all the time to maintain interest. The first year was straightforward as I was describing the things I do in a normal year, if there is such a thing. Later we started to go out to other people's gardens on a few occasions.

During 2004 we had a chap ring in to say that his front lawn had become all undulated, and when he walked across the turf it was really spongy and soft. He thought he had voles, but I suspected a mole as I couldn't see voles producing that kind of major disturbance.

'Surely you've got tell-tale mounds of earth, the classic little hills a mole makes?' I said.

'No,' he replied, 'there's no sign of earth whatsoever, which is why I think it's a vole. I've tried trapping them, I've tried this and I've tried that, but I can't seem to get rid of them.'

I said, 'Right, tell me where you live and I'll come over and have a look at the problem first-hand.' He was only about fifteen miles away, so we decided to do the next show from his front garden.

A fortnight later I turned up there, met Gwyn and his wife, and drank copious amounts of coffee. Gwyn had Anthea's mobile and I had mine, so we could have a three-way conversation on air.

Jeremy said, 'Have you looked at Gwyn's problem? What do you think it is?'

'I've looked at it and I agree with him, there *are* no mole-hills,' I said. 'But my diagnosis is still a mole, because across the road from where he lives there's a large field, and in there are literally hundreds of molehills. So somewhere along the line one of these moles has ventured across the road and settled in here without leaving its usual evidence.'

'So what are we going to do about it?'

'I've got my trusty spade with me,' I said, 'and one way to get rid of a mole is to make plenty of noise. You have to keep on slapping the lawn with the back of your spade.' And I started doing that to make convincing sounds over the radio.

'Right-ho,' he said, 'we're going to play some music now while you carry on.' I was still patting away when he came back after the record and asked, 'Have you found the mole yet?'

I said, 'No, but by now he's got a thumping headache and has probably disappeared.' Gwyn was in the background, adding his own comments. We finished the show there, and about two months later a follow-up revealed that the mole had gone, so we seemed to have solved that problem.

During the summer a guy from Swansea rang in and said, 'I have a large bungalow with a front and back garden. I've got runner beans growing in the front and they're absolutely wonderful, and I've got them growing in the back but those are all yellow and shrivelled. Can you help me?'

I said, 'It sounds like you've got two different kinds of soil for a start. What have you done to the back that you haven't done out the front?'

'Nothing,' he said. 'I dug manure into both of them.'

'Where did you get this manure?'

'From the stables.'

'Were the horses kept on hay or wood shavings?'

'Hay, I think.'

'Well, have you sprayed the beans in the back with some insecticide . . . ?'

And so on. We went through all the possible diagnoses on the programme, but the answer he kept giving me was no, no, no.

Finally I said, 'Well, I can't really fathom out why one lot in the front of the bungalow are different from those in the back, unless perhaps you've got a wind tunnel exposing and scorching the plants, whereas the others are protected.'

'No.'

'Right,' I said, 'I'll come and sort it out.'

A fortnight later I went over, opened his front gate, and there's this wonderful green and scarlet wall of flowers and fine green beans hanging everywhere; walk round the back of the bungalow and there's a large piece of ground with these crumbly brown apologies for runner beans in the middle.

So I said to Jeremy on the phone, 'Can you hear that?' I rubbed the foliage. Good runner bean foliage is silent or just audible whereas the leaves on a dying runner bean are crisp and noisy.

'Yes,' he said, 'what is it?'

I said, 'That's the sound of a happy runner bean. Now follow me,' and I walked round to the back where I made this loud scrunching noise. 'That's the sound of a dying runner bean.'

'Oh, right,' he said, 'so what's the problem?'

I had my pH meter with me, so I could measure whether the soil was acid or alkaline, and by how much (every plant has its preferred level of acidity, otherwise it becomes sick). I said I'd try the front first and that I was looking for a reading of 6.5–7.0, the ideal range for runner beans. I pushed the probe into the soil, and it said exactly 6.5. So the soil in the front was perfect.

I went round to the back and stuck the probe in the bed: 4.0!

I said, 'Well, for a start this soil is *extremely* acid and beans really don't like that. But while I was scrabbling round trying to push in the pH meter, I noticed there's all these wood shavings mixed in the soil. He's dug manure into the back garden which has come from a stable where the horse has been kept on wood shavings. What's happening is that, as the shavings are breaking down, they're exhausting the nitrogen in the soil and starving the beans.' So that's how that problem was resolved.

I've never claimed to know all the answers, though – you'd be an exceptional gardener if you had every solution at your fingertips, every plant disease that exists and the reason why certain things don't grow in certain areas. I've never considered myself to be an expert (a term I define as a combination of 'ex', someone who's past it, and 'spurt', a drip under pressure) and would rather describe myself as a practical gardener with fifty years' experience.

If I get a question on the programme that beats me, I'll always say so or try to give a humorous reply instead, which has probably added a slightly offbeat or unpredictable element to the show. For example, we had a call from a listener in Bournemouth who had a problem with his fruit. He had some raspberries and gave me their names, and a row of blackcurrants, which were growing away extremely well. But he had a new cherry with a long name that ended 'something van something'. 'I've looked everywhere,' he said, 'but I can't understand what this term "van" applies to. Can you tell me what it means?'

I said, 'Yes, that's what it was delivered in,' and then I gave a chuckle and added, 'But I don't really know.'

Sometimes it's simply impossible to give an answer on air, if you're miles from the evidence. A guy rang in once to say his leeks had all died, and asked what had gone wrong. I replied that it was a bit difficult, standing at the end of my mobile on an allotment in the Rhondda, to diagnose exactly why his leeks had died somewhere far from here. So I explained to him how I grow leeks, and then said, 'If you follow this system, they'll grow quite well here in the Rhondda. All I can suggest is that you try this next year, and if it doesn't work, move.'

In 2004 Jeremy thought we'd try growing something different, and one of the new crops was pak choi. He followed its progress as it was sown, came up, went out into the open ground and started growing quite well. Then I came on the show and said, 'Problem, Jeremy. I've got masses of little yellow flowers on the pak choi. It's obviously gone to seed, and that's the end of that. What are we going to do now?'

'Tell you what,' he said, 'we'll ask our listeners if anyone can help.'

The next time we were on, he'd had a call from someone called Winston, who sounded Caribbean. Jeremy said, 'I've got the expert on the other end of the line, Terry, and he's going to help you solve the problem with your pak choi for the future.'

I said, 'Hiya, Winston, how are you?'

Long silence. Then, 'Hi, Terry, how are you?'

'I'm fine,' I said, 'I gather you're the expert on pak choi?'

Another silence, and then, 'Yes.'

I said, 'Well, what do you do then?'

'Well, man,' he said, 'my son lives in Antigua, and every year in January he sends me over some Antiguan pak choi seed. I'm gardening in the south-east and I plant these seeds on my allotment down there, and they come up well.'

'I've done that, and they come up and always look really healthy, and then they go to seed. How do you stop them going to seed?' I asked him, expecting a simple solution.

'You don't, man. They're so used to growing in the Caribbean,' he said, 'that mine go to seed in this country as well. I've got the same problem as you!'

Things don't always go to plan on the programme because Jeremy has a strong tendency to go off at a tangent, which keeps everyone on their toes. He likes the show to be spontaneous, and most of the time I haven't got a clue what's coming next. And then you really are thinking on your feet.

I wasn't due to be on the show at all the week that Charles and Camilla got married, for example. As the event was particularly topical, they had decided to focus on that. First thing on the Friday morning before the wedding, right out of the blue, I had a call from the studio asking if I'd be available to add a comment. 'Think of something not too controversial,' they said.

So there I was, up at the allotments and listening to the show on my car radio. Various people from different Commonwealth countries were all giving their opinions about the wedding, and then Jeremy said, 'As Charles is Prince of Wales, we're now going to our adopted allotment in the Rhondda valley for the Welsh perspective. So, Terry, what do you think about this wedding?'

I said, 'Well, I'm quite happy for them at the end of the day, and he obviously seems very fond of Camilla. I'm certain she's got a hard act to follow, coming after Princess Diana who's in the heart of the country as well as the heart of the people of Wales. But she was a different character. Provided Charles and Camilla warm to the people and show them what they're like as a couple, I'm sure the people will warm to them.'

My contribution to Jeremy's programme is usually the last ten minutes of the Friday show, a kind of light-hearted wind-down into the weekend after the previous fifty minutes of serious discussion. Jeremy gets all kinds of guests in the earlier part of the show and, depending on who's preceding me, there's often some kind of overlap and interaction.

Someone I work extremely well with is Clarissa Dickson-Wright from the *Two Fat Ladies* series. She can be very outspoken, especially on topics like fox-hunting, supermarkets and green issues, and she's strongly in favour of organic allotment growing, so she usually wants to stay and be part of my bit as well.

Antony Worrall Thompson, the chef, comes on from time to time, and one Christmas Eve he was in the studio giving a cook's perspective on Christmas lunch, while I was picking produce for our own meal and explaining what I was going to do with my vegetables.

Another guest was Christine Hamilton, wife of the former MP Neil Hamilton. She called me 'Terry darling' all the time and wanted suggestions for what Neil could grow in their London flat, because he was a keen gardener with no ground to cultivate. I suggested getting a couple of growbags where he could grow salad crops like lettuce and tomatoes.

A momentous event in our lives occurred on 24 April 2004, when our granddaughter Megan Elizabeth Walton was born. She has blue eyes and blond hair, and has been able to twist her grandfather round her tiny finger from a very early age. Now I regularly experience a conflict between seeing her and going to the allotment. And, as you might guess, it's Megan who always wins.

She has been to the allotment many times and like her grandfather enjoys it there, whether she's picking strawberries or posing for her photograph while straddling one of my giant pumpkins. Who knows, perhaps if I get her interested at such an early age the family allotment tradition will be safe for another generation.

One day we had a child psychologist on the show. Jeremy has a daughter, Martha, almost exactly the same age as Megan (whom he met when he came down to the allotments). When we chat from time to time off the air or before planning a show we tend to talk about the kids and catch up on their news. After I had done my bit from the allotments on this particular occasion, Jeremy said his guest was still in the studio, and had I got any questions for her about my granddaughter?

'Yes,' I said, 'she's got to the stage now where if she starts to do something and gets frustrated, she throws things across the room.' I had a lecture then about how to prevent a child of twenty-one months from throwing. The psychologist explained that I simply had to be stern, to put on a serious voice. And Jeremy said, 'It's not easy being stern with your own granddaughter, though. Show him how to do it.' She produced this quite startling firm voice, and I said, 'God, you terrify me, *and* you'd terrify my granddaughter as well.'

About a month after I started on *The Jeremy Vine Show* in 2003, I had a call from Mish Evans, a TV producer from BBC Wales in Cardiff. She explained they were planning a new programme called *I Love Wales*.

'We're going to visit the six most famous gardens in Wales,' she said. 'There'll be a koi water garden, a peace garden and a sensory garden, a Dutch garden in Lampeter, the National Botanical Gardens of Wales and your allotment!' They were going to feature all six gardens in one special, so each would get about five minutes' coverage.

You can imagine my feelings, so soon after starting in broadcasting, to be told that Terry Walton's allotment was up there alongside the National Botanical Gardens of Wales. The presenter was Iolo Williams, who does a lot of programmes on natural history and the outdoors in Wales, and his introduction to my plot started: 'Arthur Fowler on *EastEnders* had one and Terry Walton in the Rhondda valley has got one. What is it? A famous allotment!'

Five minutes is comparatively long in a broadcast. In that time they managed to describe the plot, interview me about how I got into allotment gardening, and cover some nice stories about how I'd grown the flowers for my own wedding, and how I've been on the allotments since I was knee-high.

That was my first experience of working on a television broadcast, which is a totally different technique from radio because you are facing a camera all the time, and where you look and how you stand are important to the presenter and the cameraman. Several takes are necessary for some shots to get the effect right on screen. Also it was not live and spontaneous like the radio show, and television programmes rely on a little more acting to make them interesting. It was certainly slightly unnerving at first, but luckily lots of what is filmed always ends up on the cutting-room floor, and what was finally shown looked very good.

One of the benefits of radio is that, while your voice might be recognized, visually you are anonymous. But when people have seen your face, it's much more difficult to hide. You can be sitting in a café one day or walking through the shops and you hear the comment, 'Isn't that guy on the television?' Once you've been seen, you're public property.

HTV Wales didn't want to be left out, and soon afterwards I had a phone call from Bruce Kennedy, a producer with HTV at Culverhouse Cross in Cardiff. He said, 'You're a rising star in Wales on gardening, you seem to grow everything. We have a programme called *Grass Roots*, which covers stories about folk in Wales. Can we come along and talk to you?'

So they turned up with Hywel James, a former newscaster who now presents a lot of topical programmes like the *Good Food Show*, and they did another special seven- or eight-minute spot, covering several topics about the allotments and how I did the *Jeremy Vine* stuff. They even went along to Jeremy's studio and did a cut-in of me talking on the show.

That programme was apparently very popular, provoking so much interest in our allotments that Hywel James came back several weeks later and said, 'We'd like to do a whole series called *Going to Seed*. Not so much about gardening but more the social life on the allotments. Are there any characters beside yourself there, who you meet on a regular basis?'

I thought, well, there was Albie across the path with his glasshouse doubling up as the café; there was Russell or Nuts, our inventor; and there was Roger, a stable sort of guy who was probably the best gardener. Roger grows all the standard allotment crops – potatoes, cabbage, beans, peas, lettuce and other salad crops – as well as artichokes, fennel and lots of flowering shrubs. We became the four characters who made up the cast of the Rhondda's equivalent of *Last of the Summer Wine*.

It was a four-part series to start with. The programmes did contain gardening tips but were largely about the social interaction on the plots, together with location items at places like the Royal Agricultural Show in Cardiff Castle, where they filmed us going round the stands and meeting other allotment people, and the Royal Welsh Show in Builth Wells, where they followed us as we went round the horticultural tent.

We also went to one of the winning allotments in Cardiff, hoping to pick up some tips, although I suspect the main reason was to show viewers the contrast in tidiness between their site and ours. As we entered the place we were greeted with neatly sculpted flower borders, and there were no sheds or greenhouses to blot the landscape. The whole view was of a pristine, well-controlled site, much as ours was when I entered it fifty years ago.

Finally we did a programme with Brent Cockbain, the Welsh second row forward. He's a very keen gardener and spends much of his leisure time (when not playing rugby) on his allotment. He told us he likes to cook with his own vegetables and makes chutneys from his produce. But during the international matches that autumn he had had a very bad leg injury and was on crutches for several months, unable to dig his allotment.

The producer of *Grass Roots*, Hywel James, thought it a good idea for us allotmenteers to go on his plot and help him out, and we were digging away there when he hobbled down the path to find out what we were up to. We discussed his passion for allotment gardening and the kind of crops he had grown in his native Australia. We finished up with an impromptu coaching session for the cast, practising passing a rugby ball there on the plot.

The first series was so successful that we did another four episodes, which finished transmitting in December 2005. So we made eight shows altogether, which gave considerable exposure in Wales not just to the allotments and the members but also to the wonderful surroundings that we are privileged to enjoy every day.

During these bits and pieces of filming we were approached by a company called Liberty Bell, who were going to make a series called *Dig It* for BBC2. They wanted ten one-hour shows comparing the characters and growing methods of the Rhondda valley with a similar cast from an allotment site in Highgate in London. They planned to come along for one day a week over the full season and follow each of us growing different vegetables, monitoring our progress and results. Because it was a longer series than we'd done before, they needed a bigger cast. They chose Albie, Russell, Roger and me, who had all filmed before, plus four new faces.

Brian and his wife Myra joined the cast. I was delighted Myra could be part of the show because she was the first lady to actually work on a plot since the allotments were founded, and even though she was not the official plotholder (the plot belongs to Brian) she was planting part of it herself. This was ground-breaking stuff. A member of the opposite sex was actually running part of her husband's plot, bringing order and tidiness to this kingdom of men. It was history in the making, and where would it all end? In all seriousness we're hoping Myra's role in the show will prove to other women in our locality that there's a place for them on the allotments, and we all welcome the change.

Carl, who had only just taken a plot, was picked so they could follow his development as a novice to see if he was getting tips from everybody else. As the series progressed so did Carl's skill, and the quality of some of his vegetables put us older hands to shame. He produced one of the biggest cabbages ever grown on this site and had the nerve to parade it before us all in a large wheelbarrow.

Finally there was Rhys, a good gardener and a bit of a character, always telling jokes and making light-hearted quips about his and others' growing prowess. He didn't want to be involved at first but, once he'd started, really got a taste for it. He has been with us on the site for fifteen years and has always grown excellent vegetables, his greenhouse regularly producing the largest crop of tomatoes. If he didn't appear in one of the shows he would ring me up and ask what he had done wrong. Why didn't they want him? I would say, 'Don't worry. It's a long series, I'm sure you'll be back.' And he went on to be used a lot throughout the programmes, and has become quite a star of the small screen. So much for the reluctant volunteer!

The production team managed to build two contrasting casts of characters, with neither group knowing anything about the other one or what was taking place at the other allotments. Right through the season from April until September they filmed us at work (and play) on a fortnightly basis, one week at the Rhondda site, the next week in Highgate. Each participant was allocated a range of vegetables, and the series followed how they grew. This practical stuff was interspersed with stories of how each person got into gardening, what they liked about it and in some cases the effect it had on their life.

When filming was over the production company arranged a barbecue at the Highgate site and the Rhondda cast were bussed up to London to join the party. There was an instant affinity between us all the moment we met, which was the first time in the whole long shooting schedule, and we spent a very pleasurable day together as if we were lifelong friends. Such is the bond between fellow allotmenteers.

The show finally went out as *The Big Dig*, after a change in title at the last moment.

As a result of all my media activities the BBC Radio Wales early show *Good Morning Wales* got in touch one day to see if I would come on the programme and give my opinion about the fact daffodils were blooming much earlier these days. And I've been contributing regularly now for over two years. I think the producers sit there in the evening scanning the internet for breaking news, and if they find that something with a gardening flavour will appear in the next day's papers, they ring me up to ask my view on it. What do I think about a new law regarding *leylandii* hedges? Is it right that the grasscutters in Newcastle are going on strike because the grass there is growing in the winter? Then they'll say, 'Can you come in at ten past six tomorrow morning?'

Global change

ALL THE SCIENTIFIC EVIDENCE at the moment seems to indicate that the Earth's temperature is rising. With the exception of 2005/6, winters are definitely warmer with far fewer frosts than twenty years ago, spring tends to be wetter and cooler, and peak summer temperatures are several degrees higher. But it is the wild variations that seem to occur these days which concern gardeners more than broken records: we get very high winds at abnormal times of the year, and frosts in late May are more common now.

If the changing, warmer British climate becomes an established fact of life, allotment gardeners are going to have to reassess the kind of vegetables that can be grown well at particular times of year. Winter vegetables such as leeks, swedes and Brussels sprouts will be out and during the summer more exotics such as melons or even bananas could be grown. It might also mean we can extend the season for growing our favourite crops – who knows, later this century we might be picking runner beans and fresh strawberries to eat on Christmas Day. →

I personally don't relish the thought. I like to have clear distinctions between our four seasons, each with its appropriate weather. This helps us all to plan our gardening year and grow accordingly. We allotmenteers are a staid bunch, really, and prefer change to be minimal.

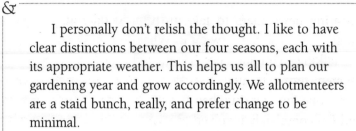

The questions may not be purely about gardening but there's always a link somewhere, which is why I'm called in to provide a comment. Barring the fact that I've got to get up at some ridiculous hour to go to the studio, I don't mind: everybody's got an opinion on something, but I'm lucky enough to be able to express mine on air.

And it's all based on what I do or have learned on the allotment. Whether I'm describing my attempts to grow tomatillo or skirret on my plot, sharing a laugh and a joke with my fellow plotholders on television, or simply giving my views on early morning radio about the health-promoting properties of rhubarb, it's all just a natural (even if totally unexpected) consequence of enjoying gardening and wanting to share its pleasures with others.

All my initial misgivings about featuring allotment gardening on the radio have proved to be unfounded. I'm still nervous before each broadcast – some things never change! – but that keeps me sharp, which translates into good listening. The routine that has evolved between Jeremy and me obviously appeals to our audience, who keep tuning in regularly, and the fan mail I receive suggests it has hit the right note with Radio 2 gardeners. Long may the programme continue inspiring newcomers to take up this wonderful pastime of ours!

Talking to an audience has made me see the allotment in different terms, though. I seldom stand back and look at the plot while I'm working, because it's there in my mind already and I'm completely involved in whatever I'm doing. But when I describe it to other people, such as Jeremy Vine's millions of listeners, and try to ensure they get the feel of it, then I have to look at it as a whole.

I think I appreciate it even more now, if that's possible.

As time passes, the adopted allotment, my patch of good earth on this mountainside overlooking the stunning Rhondda valley, seems to me even more like a small piece of heaven. And the plot has turned out to be much more fruitful than anyone could have predicted when I first joined my father up there over half a century ago.

Who could have foreseen that my secret haven of peace and solitude would now be shared with six million listeners? Like nature, life is full of surprises, some good, some bad, and many of my richest pleasures have come from owning my own allotment and growing my own food.

So here's to the next fifty years on my hillside in the Rhondda.

Terry's Tip for December

Recycling

To save on the cost of new pots for sowing and growing next year's crops, *and* to help reduce the huge amounts of waste we generate, get friendly with someone who works at a place with a drinks-vending machine, preferably one that dispenses polystyrene cups.

Collect these and wash them out in hot soapy water, and then burn a half-inch (12 mm) hole in the bottoms with a soldering iron to provide drainage. You can use these 'pots' for germinating large seeds like beans, sweetcorn and sunflowers, and for growing on seedlings to make decent-size plants for transplanting outdoors. The polystyrene keeps the plants warm and cosy, and doesn't dry out as fast as conventional plastics.

You can use the stuff elsewhere too. Save all the polystyrene packing from Christmas presents and break it into small pieces to use as drainage material at the bottom of pots. Larger polystyrene containers make excellent seed trays or 'saucers' for standing under pots to catch water.

Remember you can use other waste materials in the garden too. Clear plastic containers that meat and fish are sold in make effective propagator lids over trays of seedlings or cuttings, and all your Christmas wrapping paper can be ripped up small to add carbon to the vegetable waste in your compost bin.

Anthea's Recipe for December

Green Tomato Chutney

*W*HEN THE FIRST AUTUMN FROST *is forecast, harvest all your remaining tomatoes and lay them out in trays indoors to finish ripening. Adding a ripe banana or an orange helps speed up the process. If you have lots of green ones that look as if they're never going to turn red, this recipe will use up quite a few of them.*

- 2 lb (900 g) green tomatoes, chopped small
- ¼ lb (225 g) onions, chopped small
- ¼ pint (150 ml) water
- ¼ pint (150 ml) malt vinegar
- 12 oz (350 g) jar orange marmalade
- 4 oz (125 g) mixed raisins and sultanas
- 1 tsp cayenne pepper
- ½ tsp ground ginger
- ½ tsp salt

Simmer water and onions in a large saucepan for 20 mins.

Add tomatoes, vinegar, sultanas and raisins, spices and salt, and simmer for 25 mins.

Melt the marmalade slowly in a saucepan or a microwave on the lowest power. Add to the tomato mixture and stir to mix thoroughly.

Spoon into preheated jars and cover at once with airtight lids.

Ode to the Allotment

I once had an allotment that was all mine,
Now I share it with the listeners of Jeremy Vine.
It resides in the Rhondda valley in a beautiful spot,
And I'm very thankful for the view that I've got.

When life is tough and I'm feeling a bit low
I jump in the car and to the allotment I go;
I meet all the characters on their plots too,
And after a chat and a coffee I no longer feel blue.

It is great to work there, and also sit and stare,
And admire all the crops that are growing there.
We meet in Albie's greenhouse, sunshine or rain,
And after a chat the world is put to right again.

It provides in the summer the salad on my plate -
The lettuce, radish, tomatoes and 'cues' are great.
On colder days the hot dinners are just fine
With potatoes, carrots, cabbage and beans divine.

To add to my taste buds courgettes and sweetcorn
These wonderful vegetables my dinner plate adorn,
My winter feasts provided by parsnip, leek and swede;
So you see the allotment provides all that I need.

Then I moved on to pumpkins that grew quite large,
To see them many people to my plot would charge.
There are failures, of course – the pak choi is one:
The plants went to seed, so its fruitful days were done.

The strawberry, gooseberry and blackberry I farm
To provide desserts on my plate and tasty jam.
So you see I have all that I need in my life:
Allotment, beautiful views, two great sons . . . and a
    patient wife!

Index